B1
SCRATCH
YOUR BRAIN
CLEVER MATH TICKLERS

SERIES TITLES:
SCRATCH YOUR BRAIN A1
SCRATCH YOUR BRAIN B1
SCRATCH YOUR BRAIN C1
SCRATCH YOUR BRAIN ALGEBRA
SCRATCH YOUR BRAIN GEOMETRY

DOUG BRUMBAUGH

LINDA BRUMBAUGH

DAVID ROCK

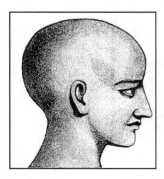

© 2001
THE CRITICAL THINKING CO.
(BRIGHT MINDS™)
www.CriticalThinking.com
P.O. Box 1610 • Seaside • CA 93955-1610
Phone 800-458-4849 • FAX 831-393-3277
ISBN 0-89455-789-0
Printed in the Unites States of America

D1377712

CONTENTS ────────────────────────────────

INTRODUCTION

This book contains 180 problems, all of which meet at least one of the standards set forth by the National Council of Teachers of Mathematics. The next two pages contain matrices that link each problem to its relevant standards. The problems are sequenced by difficulty throughout the book and each chapter. Chapter titles correspond to common textbook topics.

Many of the problems in this book also ask students to write explanations of how they got their answers. Scoring rubrics are included for each of these problems. Keep in mind that students will often come up with an answer that is not totally correct but still shows the thinking necessary to obtain the correct answer. Thus, a student could get "partial credit" even though the final answer is not correct. This partial credit would be the recognition that the student was able to articulate through words and sentences the mathematical processes one would use to arrive at the correct answer.

For example, problem 41 on page 24 says this:

41. When you add the digits of the 2-digit multiples of 7 (14, 21, 28,...), some of them add to ten (from 28, 2 + 8 = 10). What is the sum of the 2-digit multiples of seven whose digits have a sum of ten?

Write an explanation of how you got your answer.

Here is a sample student answer:

I listed the two-digit multiples of 7: 14, 21, 28, 35, 42, 49, 56, 63, 70, 77, 84, 91, and 98. Two multiples, 28 and 91, have digits that add to 10. I added these two multiples. Their sum is 119.

Here is the rubric for this problem (page 110):

Rubric: 4 possible points
1 point (content): Know the multiples of 7
1 point (content): Know which multiples of 7 to select
1 point (content): Correct arithmetic
1 point (clarity): The explanation is clearly written

The sample student answer shows the multiples of 7 and which multiples of 7 to select. The arithmetic is correct and the explanation of how the problem was solved is clearly written. Thus, this answer would be worth the full 4 points. A student who knew the multiples of 7 and which multiples of 7 to select, but did not use the correct arithmetic or clearly articulate the steps needed to solve the problem, would be awarded 2 points. (At the teacher's discretion, 1 point could be awarded for a clear explanation of how an incorrect answer was derived. This might not seem plausible on an easier problem, but more difficult problems could lend themselves to this possibility.)

ACTIVITIES ACCORDING TO
NATIONAL MATHEMATICS STANDARDS

NCTM Standard	1	2	3	4	5	6	7	8	9	10	11	12	13	14	15	16	17	18	19	20	21	22	23	24	25	26	27	28	29	30	31	32	33	34	35	36
Number, Operation	■	■						■	■	■		■		■	■			■	■	■	■	■	■	■		■	■	■		■	■	■	■	■	■	■
Algebra																								■							■			■		
Geometry			■																																	
Measurement																	■	■		■								■	■		■			■	■	
Data Analysis, Probability																	■																			
Problem Solving		■	■	■	■	■	■	■	■	■	■	■	■	■	■	■	■	■	■	■	■			■	■	■	■	■	■	■	■	■	■	■	■	■
Reasoning, Proof		■	■	■	■	■	■				■	■	■	■	■	■	■	■	■	■			■	■	■	■	■	■	■	■	■	■	■	■	■	■
Communication											■							■														■				■
Connections							■		■					■				■		■	■			■				■	■				■	■	■		■
Representation		■	■		■	■	■				■	■	■		■	■	■			■				■		■	■	■	■	■	■	■	■	■	■	

NCTM Standard	37	38	39	40	41	42	43	44	45	46	47	48	49	50	51	52	53	54	55	56	57	58	59	60	61	62	63	64	65	66	67	68	69	70	71	72
Number, Operation		■	■	■	■	■	■	■	■	■	■	■		■	■	■	■	■	■	■	■	■			■	■	■								■	
Algebra		■	■					■				■							■	■																
Geometry																								■								■				
Measurement													■			■												■	■	■	■	■			■	■	■
Data Analysis, Probability																																				
Problem Solving	■	■	■	■	■	■	■	■			■	■	■	■	■	■	■	■	■	■	■	■	■	■	■	■	■		■	■	■	■	■	■	■	■
Reasoning, Proof	■	■	■		■	■		■	■		■	■	■	■	■	■	■	■	■	■	■	■	■	■	■	■	■		■	■	■	■	■	■	■	■
Communication					■								■							■												■			■	■
Connections		■	■	■	■				■		■	■		■	■	■	■			■	■	■			■		■					■			■	■
Representation		■					■						■	■		■				■	■	■		■			■		■	■	■	■	■	■	■	■

NCTM Standard	73	74	75	76	77	78	79	80	81	82	83	84	85	86	87	88	89	90	91	92	93	94	95	96	97	98	99	100	101	102	103	104	105	106	107
Number, Operation		■						■		■	■	■			■	■	■	■	■		■	■		■	■	■	■	■	■	■	■	■			■
Algebra		■																				■								■					
Geometry										■															■										
Measurement	■	■	■	■			■	■	■	■	■	■	■	■					■	■		■										■	■	■	■
Data Analysis, Probability																										■					■				
Problem Solving	■	■	■	■	■	■	■	■	■	■	■	■	■	■	■	■	■	■	■	■	■	■	■	■	■	■	■	■	■	■	■	■	■	■	■
Reasoning, Proof	■	■	■	■	■	■	■	■	■	■		■	■	■		■		■	■	■	■	■	■	■	■	■	■	■	■	■	■	■	■	■	■
Communication		■	■																			■			■					■		■			
Connections			■							■	■		■	■	■				■			■			■	■				■	■	■	■		■
Representation	■		■	■	■	■			■	■		■		■	■	■	■		■	■		■	■		■		■			■		■	■	■	■

ACTIVITIES ACCORDING TO
NATIONAL MATHEMATICS STANDARDS

NCTM Standard	108	109	110	111	112	113	114	115	116	117	118	119	120	121	122	123	124	125	126	127	128	129	130
Number, Operation	■				■	■	■			■				■			■			■		■	■
Algebra																			■				
Geometry		■		■				■	■	■	■	■	■	■	■	■	■	■	■	■	■		
Measurement	■			■	■		■										■				■		
Data Analysis, Probability		■		■																			
Problem Solving	■	■	■	■	■	■	■	■	■	■	■	■	■	■	■	■	■	■	■	■	■	■	■
Reasoning, Proof	■	■	■	■	■	■	■	■	■	■	■	■	■	■	■	■	■	■	■	■	■	■	
Communication			■																			■	
Connections	■	■		■	■		■		■	■	■	■	■	■	■	■	■			■	■	■	
Representation	■	■			■	■	■			■		■		■	■		■	■	■	■		■	

NCTM Standard	131	132	133	134	135	136	137	138	139	140	141	142	143	144	145	146	147	148	149	150	151	152	153	154	155
Number, Operation	■	■	■	■	■	■	■	■	■	■	■	■	■	■	■	■		■	■	■	■	■	■	■	
Algebra							■						■									■			
Geometry						■								■	■				■						
Measurement				■			■	■		■							■							■	
Data Analysis, Probability																					■				
Problem Solving	■	■	■	■	■	■	■	■	■	■	■	■		■	■	■	■	■	■	■	■	■	■	■	■
Reasoning, Proof		■	■	■	■	■	■	■	■	■	■	■	■		■	■	■	■	■	■	■	■		■	■
Communication																						■			
Connections	■	■	■	■	■			■		■		■	■		■	■	■	■			■	■	■	■	
Representation		■	■	■	■		■		■		■	■			■		■				■		■	■	

NCTM Standard	156	157	158	159	160	161	162	163	164	165	166	167	168	169	170	171	172	173	174	175	176	177	178	179	180
Number, Operation											■													■	■
Algebra																								■	
Geometry																								■	
Measurement																									
Data Analysis, Probability																								■	
Problem Solving	■	■	■	■	■	■	■	■	■	■	■	■	■	■	■	■	■	■	■	■	■	■	■	■	■
Reasoning, Proof	■	■	■	■	■	■	■	■	■	■		■	■	■	■	■	■	■	■	■	■	■	■	■	■
Communication		■		■		■	■			■		■			■		■	■		■		■			
Connections						■																			
Representation	■	■					■	■	■	■	■	■			■			■	■		■	■		■	

Place Value and Money ⸻⸻⸻⸻⸻⸻⸻⸻

1. How many numbers are there between 1 and 100 that have at least one 9 in them?

2. Which number becomes larger when turned upside down?

3. There is a line of cars with 4 cars ahead of a car and a car in the middle. What is the fewest number of cars in line?

4. You have 2 U.S. coins in your pocket. Their total value is 15 cents. One coin is not a dime. What are your two coins?

© 2001 Critical Thinking Books & Software • www.criticalthinking.com • 800-458-4849

5. NOTE TO TEACHER: A student will think of a number and other students will take turns asking questions that may be answered with only YES or NO. For example, a student might ask, "Is it even? Is it greater than 1000? Does it contain a 4?" This continues until 20 questions have been asked. The student who guesses the number correctly will be the next one to think of a new number to guess. If the correct number is not guessed in 20 questions, the student tells the number and then gets to pick another number for the others to guess.

6. If you take 5 coins from a piggy bank containing 17 coins, how many coins would you have?

7. Which is worth more—a new ten dollar bill or an old one?

8. What is the smallest whole number that uses the letter A in its English spelling?

9. Using U.S. currency, how many different ways can you pay 25 cents? (A quarter is different from two dimes and a nickel, even though they both have a total value of 25 cents.) List each of the possible ways to do this.

10. What comes next in the sequence?

st, nd, rd, th, _____, _____

11. Continue the pattern: t, f, s, e, t, t, f, s, _____, _____

12. In a hardware store, a person buys a particular type of item. When the purchase is made, 1 would cost $1, 50 would cost $2, and 200 would cost $3. What is being purchased?

13. Jonesy gave Forty three dollars for some wood, and then sold it for $50. What was the profit?

14. How many times does each digit from 0–9 appear in a list of whole numbers from 0 to 100 inclusive?

Write an explanation of how you got your answer.

_____

_____

_____

_____

15. How many whole numbers less than 1000 contain at least one 2 but no 3s?

Write an explanation of how you got your answer.

_____

_____

_____

_____

16. How much money would you have if you had 2 female pigs and 2 male deer?

17. How many birthdays does the average person have?

18. You have exactly $4.40 in United States quarters, dimes, and nickels. How many of each coin do you have if you have the exact same number of each type of coin?

Write an explanation of how you got your answer.

_____

_____

_____

_____

19. Ask a student to hold a dime in one hand and a penny in the other. Tell the student to multiply the value of the coin in the right hand by 8, and then multiply the value of the other coin by 5. The student is to add the results and tell you the sum. You will then identify which coin is in which hand. Students can write an explanation of how they solved the problem.

20. You have six coins in your pocket totaling $1.15, yet you cannot make change for a dollar, half dollar, quarter, dime, or nickel. What coins do you have in your pocket?

21. Using U.S currency, how many different ways can you pay 50 cents? (Two quarters are different from five dimes, even though they both have a total value of 50 cents.) List each of the possible ways to do this.

22. Divide the class into teams of up to 8 players. Each team should have the same number of players. If one team is short, they select someone to go twice. On the command "go," the first student in each team goes to the board and writes a number. The chalk is given to the next player in line to do the same. Play continues until all but one player remains on each team. The last player on each team will write the sum of the column of numbers written by the team members. A point is awarded to the team if the sum is correct. Players rotate and a second round is played. A game is determined when each player on the team has had one chance to add the column (unless a player has to go twice).

23. Some kids had 10 pizzas and ate all but two. How many pizzas did they have left?

24. Students will choose a secret number between 1 and 100, then follow your directions carefully. You will be able to tell them what number they have when they finish.

Directions:

Pick a number.

Add 10 to your number.

Double the sum.

Add 100.

Take half of the result or sum.

Subtract the number you started with.

Variation: When the computations are finished, go around the room asking each student what number they ended up with, acting surprised that more and more of them have 60. Watch their amazement!

25. There are 7 numbers that are not even. Their sum is 13. The greatest number is 7. What are the numbers?

26. What digit should replace the question mark in the grid of numbers?

5	3	7	8	9
2	6	4	1	?
8	0	2	0	4

27. A sixty-page newspaper, which consists of only one section, has the sheet with page 12 missing. There are 4 pages on a sheet. What other pages are missing?

Write an explanation of how you got your answer.

_____

_____

_____

_____

28. You have three and only three containers: 10 units, 4 units, and 3 units. The 10-unit container is full of water and you have no other water available. You are to divide the water so there is exactly 5 units in the 10-unit container, 1 unit in the 3-unit container, and 4 units in the 4-unit container. (You may only pour back and forth between the three given containers, and there are no unit measurements on the containers.) What is the fewest number of pours it will take to accomplish the task?

Write an explanation of how you got your answer.

_____

_____

_____

_____

29. Each tire for my monster truck will last exactly 14,000 miles. How many spares do I need so I can use the fewest number of tires in a total of 21,000 miles?

Write an explanation of how you got your answer.

_____

_____

_____

_____

30. Remove exactly 5 digits from the expression

$$111 + 333 + 777 + 999$$

so that the remaining numbers will sum to 1111.

31. How many pigs and ducks are in the pen if there is a total of 17 heads and 50 feet?

32. Have a student add 3 dates from a vertical column on a calendar, and tell you the answer. You can then tell the student the three dates selected.

Variation: Have each student select and then total their own 3 dates, and you can tell each of them the numbers in their list.

33. NOTE TO TEACHER: Read aloud one sentence at a time. Students will compute, then wait for the next sentence.

Take the number of fingers and thumbs on one hand. Multiply that by the number of nickels in a quarter. Add the number of players on a baseball team to your answer. (If necessary, explain that you mean the number of active players on the non-batting team.) Now add the number of centimeters in a meter to that answer.

34. Ask a student to pick any three consecutive dates on a calendar and show them to the class so you cannot see the numbers. Ask the class to add these three values and tell you the sum. Then you tell the students the second of the 3 dates they have selected.

35. Have a student select 4 consecutive dates on a calendar, and show them to the class without showing you. Have the class find the sum of those 4 dates. The students tell you their sum. You tell them the 4 dates selected.

Variation: Have each student select their own 4 consecutive dates and you can still tell each of them the second date in their list.

36. The sum of the weights of a dog and a cat is 27 pounds. The dog weighs an odd number of pounds. Each animal's weight is a counting number. If he weighs twice as much as she does, what are the weights of the dog and the cat?

37. Announce your ability to remember numbers. Ask your students to copy the group of numbers below exactly as they appear. Tell the students to choose one line from the list below and erase the appropriate digit(s) from the array of numbers on the board while your back is turned. Then say that you will be able to replace the missing digit(s) when you turn around.

8	6	4	2	7	5	4
6	7	2	8	5	7	1
5	4	9	3	3	4	8
1	9	3	2	5	9	7
3	4	6	7	6	4	6
4	5	5	6	8	1	7
9	1	7	8	2	6	3

Any one digit

Any two digits

Any three digits

Any one digit in each row

Any one digit in each column

Any one digit in each diagonal

     All the digits in one column

     All the digits in one row

     All the digits in one diagonal

     All the digits in one row and one diagonal

     All the digits in one column and one diagonal

38. Suppose students arrive at school in groups. You are the first to arrive and you are alone but still considered a group. The second group to arrive has three people in it—two more people in it than are in your group. The third group has five people in it—two more people than are in the second group. If there are 625 kids at your school on this day, how many groups will arrive at school, assuming they all meet the requirement of having two more members than the one before them?

```
              HOMESCHOOL HANGOUT
                162 MARIETTA ST
              ALPHARETTA, GA 30004


    TERMINAL I.D.:              067600

    MERCHANT #:         27250018093501

    VISA
    ************4448
    SALE
    BATCH: 001170      INVOICE: 000007
    DATE: SEP 02, 11      TIME: 14:31
    RRN: 11700007      AUTH NO: 00240B



    TOTAL              $17.11


    VAISHALI TRIVEDI


            CUSTOMER COPY
```

39.   Suppose you are adding three counting numbers, each of which is less than 10. We will call the three numbers we are adding A, B, and C. If the sum is AB (a 2-digit number), and A is one, what must C always be, no matter what value you have for B?

40.   If you add the consecutive counting numbers starting with one, what number of counting numbers will make the sum equal to or more than 1,000?

Write an explanation of how you got your answer.

_____

_____

_____

_____

41. When you add the digits of the 2-digit multiples of 7 (14, 21, 28,...), some of them add to ten (from 28, 2 + 8 = 10). What is the sum of the 2-digit multiples of seven whose digits have a sum of ten?

Write an explanation of how you got your answer.

_____

_____

_____

_____

42. The numbers in each of the triangles have something in common. Use the information from each triangle to determine the missing number in the last triangle.

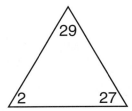
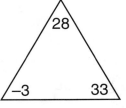
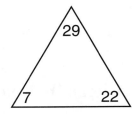
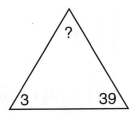

43.   Find the digit represented by each of the letters A, B, and C. Each letter must represent a unique digit, and A cannot equal zero.

$$
\begin{array}{r}
A\ B\ C \\
A\ B\ C \\
+\ A\ B\ C \\
\hline
B\ B\ B
\end{array}
$$

Write an explanation of how you got your answer.

_____

_____

_____

_____

_____

_____

_____

44. Replace the letters with the counting numbers 1 through 10. Each counting number is to be used only once. Each letter must be the difference of the two above it, one above right and the other above left. That is,

$$E = A - B \text{ or } B - A,$$

$$K = H - J \text{ or } J - H, \text{ etc.}$$

```
   A      B      C      D

      E      F      G

         H      J

            K
```

MULTIPLICATION AND DIVISION ——————

45. Look for patterns in the ones and tens places of the sums and products below. Look up, and then look down.

9 + 1 = 10	9 x 1 = 9 (09)
9 + 2 = 11	9 x 2 = 18
9 + 3 = 12	9 x 3 = 27
9 + 4 = 13	9 x 4 = 36
9 + 5 = 14	9 x 5 = 45
9 + 6 = 15	9 x 6 = 54
9 + 7 = 16	9 x 7 = 63
9 + 8 = 17	9 x 8 = 72
9 + 9 = 18	9 x 9 = 81

Explain the pattern on the lines below.

_____

_____

_____

_____

46. Which of the following numbers are not prime? Arrange the numbers that are not prime in ascending order on the line segments below (smallest to largest).

1	11	41	91	101	131	151	171	181
2	23	43	73	83	103	143	153	163
37	67	97	107	117	127	137	167	187
59	79	89	109	119	139	149	169	179

_____

_____

_____

47. Have the students choose a secret number and perform the following operations on it as instructed:

Pick a number

Triple it

Add 36

Divide by 3

Subtract the original number

You will be able to guess their number!

48. Three times a certain number plus 6 is twenty more than that certain number. What is the missing number?

49. If you stand on the scale with both feet and weigh 75 pounds, what will you weigh standing with only one foot on the scale?

Write an explanation of how you got your answer.

_____

_____

_____

_____

50. NOTE TO TEACHER: Read aloud one sentence at a time. Students will compute, then wait for the next sentence.

Take the number of ears on a dog. Multiply that number by the number of feet on a dog. Divide that number by the number of tails on a dog. Add the number of eyes on a dog.

51. Complete the following pattern. Predict the next three lines.

$$1 \times 8 + 1 = 9$$

$$12 \times 8 + 2 = 98$$

$$123 \times 8 + 3 = 987$$

$$1234 \times 8 + 4 = 9876$$

$$12345 \times 8 + 5 = 98765$$

$$123456 \times 8 + 6 = 987654$$

52. If it costs 25 cents to make a straight cut on a board, how much will it cost to cut that board into 7 pieces?

Write an explanation of how you got your answer.

_____

_____

_____

_____

53. A number is perfect if its factors (excluding the number itself) sum to the number itself. The first perfect number is 6 because its factors of 1, 2, and 3 (exclude 6) give a sum of 6. The next perfect number is 28 because $1 + 2 + 4 + 7 + 14 = 28$. What is the next perfect number? HINT—It has 3 digits.

54. Each row of numbers contains factors and products. Search for number sentences and draw loops around those you locate. (Look from left to right.) For example, you might get something like the following:

3 4 5 2 0 9

4 x 5 = 20

0 4 2 8 6 7 4 2 9 1 9 7

6 6 5 3 0 0 9 0 9 8 7 2

5 7 3 5 8 4 3 2 7 3 2 1

2 2 4 5 3 1 5 4 7 2 8 1

55. Take any multiple of three, sum the cubes of its digits, take the result, sum the cubes of its digits, take the results, etc. You will eventually get to a number that will keep repeating. What is that number? For example,

612 gives $6^3 + 1^3 + 2^3 = 225$

225 gives $2^3 + 2^3 + 5^3 = 141$, etc.

56. Maria and Manuel are on the first floor of an office building that has 50 floors. Maria takes an elevator to the 25th floor. Manuel takes a different elevator that stops at the 5th floor.

Write an explanation, in terms of elevator travel, of how much farther Maria has traveled.

_____

_____

_____

_____

_____

_____

57. NOTE TO TEACHER: Read aloud one sentence at a time. Students will compute, then wait for the next sentence.

Take the number of oranges in a dozen. Add the number of inches in a yard to that. Subtract the number of months in a year from that answer. Now divide by the number of quarts in a gallon.

58. NOTE TO TEACHER: Read aloud one sentence at a time. Students will compute, then wait for the next sentence.

Take the number of ounces in a pound. Divide that number by the sum of your eyes and ears. Multiply your answer by the number of inches in a foot. Now add the number of dimes in a dollar. What do you have?

59. What kind of tires do math teachers put on their cars?

60. What do all of the letters "B, D, E, F, H, K, L, M, N, P, R" have in common that none of the other letters in the English alphabet have?

61. One and nine are two of five counting numbers that give a sum of 25. Those same five numbers, when multiplied together, give a product of 945. What are the other 3 numbers?

62. Determine the values of A, B, C, and D, which are all counting numbers, given the following:

$A \times B = 24$

$A + B = 14$

$C \times D = 48$

$A \times D = 192$

$B \times C = 6$

63. What is the smallest number of marbles when

grouping by 4s leaves 2 extra,

grouping by 5s leaves 1 extra,

and more than 10 marbles are in the collection?

64. How can a raw egg drop 5 feet without breaking?

65. If there are twelve 1-cent stamps in a dozen, how many 29-cent stamps are there in a dozen?

66. Where do math teachers shop?

67. A runner ran 6 miles in 75 minutes when wearing Speedy Sneakers. When wearing Rapid Racers, it took the runner an hour and 15 minutes to run the same distance. How could this be true?

68. How long will it take a mile-long train going 15 miles per hour to go through and completely out of a mile-long tunnel?

Write an explanation of how you got your answer.

_____

_____

_____

69. If you set your alarm clock for 9:00 and go to bed at 8:00, how many hours of sleep will you get—assuming you fall asleep right away?

70. How many feet are in a yard?

71. Suppose someone gives you 3 bags, 2 of which contain fool's gold weighing 1 ounce per nugget and the third containing real gold weighing 1.1 ounce per nugget. You are permitted 1 weighing to determine which bag contains the real gold. How can it be done?

Write an explanation of how you got your answer.

_____

_____

_____

_____

72. Your vet gives you 3 pills for your sick dog Rover. You are to give Rover one pill every half hour. How long will the pills last?

Write an explanation of how you got your answer.

_____

_____

_____

_____

73. If an empty barrel weighs 20 pounds, what can you put in that barrel to make it weigh less?

74. Suppose you have several unit cubes (1 by 1 by 1) stacked together to make one big cube that is 5 by 5 by 5. If each of the shaded corner cubes (you cannot see all of them) is removed, what is the surface area of the remaining figure?

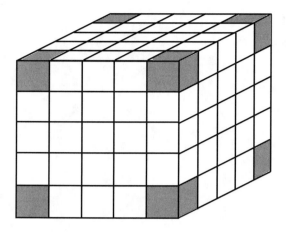

Write an explanation of how you got your answer.

_____

_____

_____

75. What did the alien from the planet Metric say to the Earthling?

76. Why is a giant's hand only 11 inches long?

77. At what time between 7:00 and 8:00 will the hands of a clock be on a straight line?

78. If you set your alarm clock for 9 A.M. and go to bed at 8:00 P.M., how many hours of sleep will you get—providing you fall asleep right away?

79. If a clock chimes 6 times in five seconds, how many times will it chime in ten seconds? State a rule for doing this problem if you can.

Write an explanation of how you got your answer.

_____

_____

_____

_____

80. There is one in every minute, one in each month, only two in next millennium, yet only one in a million years. What is it?

Write an explanation of how you got your answer.

_____

_____

_____

_____

81. Some months have 30 days. Some months have 31 days. How many months have 28 days?

82. What is the distance around the figure? Assume all angles are right angles. Do not assume that line segments which appear to be the same length actually are, or that the figure is drawn to scale.

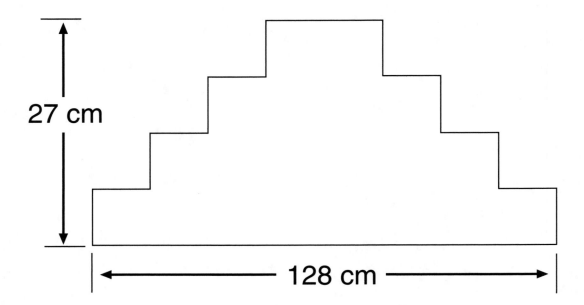

27 cm

128 cm

83. The winner of a talent contest is announced at 4:00 P.M. One person calls 2 friends before 4:15 P.M., telling the name of the winner. Before 4:30, those 2 people call 2 more and tell them the name of the winner. Before 4:45 P.M., each new person who has been called calls 2 more people, telling them the name of the winner. By about what time will at least 200 people know the name of the winner?

84. If a year is 365.25 days long, how many seconds are represented by

5 years, 21 days, 4 hours, 32 minutes, 17 seconds

− 2 years, 93 days, 7 hours, 47 minutes, 24 seconds

85. A child was born in Boston, Massachusetts to parents who were both born in Boston, Massachusetts. The child was not automatically a United States citizen.

How is this possible?

86. Town A is 5 hours from Town B by train. Trains leave A every hour on the hour headed for B. Trains leave B every hour on the half-hour headed for A. As you ride from A to B, how many trains bound from B to A would you pass?

Write an explanation of how you got your answer.

_____

_____

_____

_____

87. A man is born on March 10, 29 B.C. He dies on March 9, A.D. 41. How old was the man on the day he died?

Write an explanation of how you determined your answer.

_____

_____

_____

_____

88. Imagine looking at a digital clock that shows only hours and minutes. How many different readings between 11:00 A.M. and 5:00 P.M. of the same day will contain at least two 2s in the time?

89. Insert one and only one line segment (like a dash "—") in "15 10 5" so the new statement is equal to 4:45.

90. The numerical format for November 19, 1999 is 11-19-1999. Notice that all of the digits are odd. April 13, 1989 (4-13-1989) has both even and odd digits, thus, this date is neither odd nor even. February 2, 2000 (2-2-2000) is an even date since all digits are even.

What will be the first odd date after November 19, 1999? What was the last even date before February 2, 2000? You must identify both dates correctly.

91. Every hour, on the hour, a bus leaves town A and heads toward town B. Every hour, on the hour, another bus leaves town B and heads toward town A. The trip between the two towns takes exactly two hours. How many buses going from town A to town B will the people on a bus going from town B to town A see during their trip? Assume there are no accidents or delays and that all buses are on time leaving and arriving.

Write an explanation of how you got your answer.

_____

_____

_____

_____

92. What is the next letter in the sequence?

S, M, H, D, W, M, ____

Using Data, Ratio, Percent, and Probability

93. Find the next two terms in the series below.

9, 18, 11, 16, 13, 14, 15, 12, 17, 10, _____, _____

Write an explanation of how you got your answer.

_____

_____

_____

94. What would be the next two counting numbers in the sequence 2, 7, 12, 5, 10, 3, _____, _____ ?

Write an explanation of how you got your answer.

_____

_____

_____

95. Complete the following pattern:

J, F, M, A, M, J, J, A, ____, _____, ____, D

Write an explanation of how you got your answer.

_____

_____

_____

_____

96. Determine the value for ✳ in the following list of numbers:

12, 4, 7, 9, 15, 2, ✳, 10, 13, 5

97. Find the next two numbers in the given sequence.

$$2, 3, 10, 12, 13, 20, \underline{\hspace{1cm}}, \underline{\hspace{1cm}}$$

Write an explanation of how you got your answer.

_____

_____

_____

_____

_____

98. One red, one white, and one blue marble are in a box. In another box are seven pieces of paper, each one having one day of the week written on it. You get one chance to pick from one box. If you draw a blue marble or a weekend day (Saturday or Sunday), you get to be excused from one quiz. Which box offers you the best chance of getting out of a quiz?

Write an explanation of how you got your answer.

_____

_____

_____

_____

_____

99. The picture shows a honeycomb with the Queen bee in the center.

How many nests touch the Queen's nest?

How many nests touch a nest that touches the Queen's nest?

If the nests touching the Queen's nest are called neighborhood 1, and the nests touching the nests that touch the Queen's nest are called neighborhood 2, how many nests are in neighborhood 3, neighborhood 4, and neighborhood 5? How many nests will be in neighborhood N?

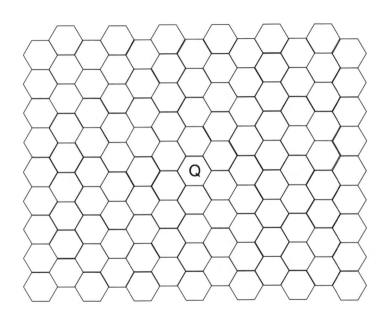

Write an explanation of how you got your answer.

_____

_____

_____

100. What is the next element in the set?

{1, 8, 18, 80, 81, 82, 83, 84, 85, 86, 87, 88, 89, 100, _____}

101. Player A chooses a counting number that is 10 or less. Player B adds any counting number between 1 and 10 to the number Player A chose. The players take turns choosing counting numbers between 1 and 10 and adding them to the previous sum until they reach the sum of 100. The winner is the first to say 100 or more.

102. In the rows shown, the middle number in any odd-numbered row (with the top row being row number 1) is the square of the row number.

What is the middle entry of the 23rd row?

What is the sum of all the entries in the 10th row?

$$1$$

$$3 \quad 5$$

$$7 \quad 9 \quad 11$$

$$13 \quad 15 \quad 17 \quad 19$$

$$21 \quad 23 \quad 25 \quad 27 \quad 29$$

Write an explanation of how you got your answer.

_____

_____

_____

_____

103. There are three children in a family. The oldest is 15. The average of their ages is 11. The median* age is 10. How old is the youngest child?

*median: the middle number when numbers are arranged in order of size. If there is no middle number, then take the average of the two middle numbers.

Write an explanation of how you got your answer.

_____

_____

_____

_____

104. The phone company has 25 computer-controlled switching systems. Each system handles 700,000 calls an hour. Each system works correctly 95% of the time. How many calls WOULD NOT BE CORRECTLY handled in one 24-hour period, assuming each of the 25 systems was running at maximum capacity at all times?

Write an explanation of how you got your answer.

_____

_____

_____

_____

105. Here are some towers made out of cubes.

Assuming the pattern continues, answer the following:

How many cubes high will Tower 1234 be?

How many cubes long will each wing in Tower 427 be?

How many cubes will it take to build Tower 873?

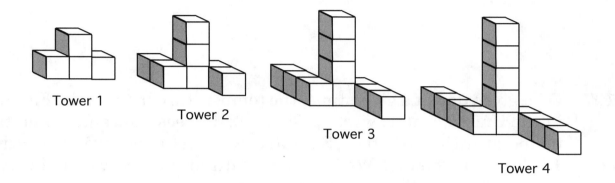

Tower 1

Tower 2

Tower 3

Tower 4

106. 7J, 4F, 4M, 1A, 6M, 3J, 1J, 5A, 2S, 7O, _____, _____

107. On a given day at a given time, the temperature in Orlando, Florida, in the United States, was a positive 82 degrees Fahrenheit and the temperature in Saskatoon, Saskatchewan, in Canada was a negative 17 degrees Celsius. What was the difference between the two temperatures at that time on that day?

108. Suppose you purchased a $60 item at 40% off and a $40 item at 20% off. What percent discount did you get on the total purchase?

Write an explanation of how you got your answer.

_____

_____

_____

_____

_____

_____

109. You live at A on the picture below and a friend lives at B. Assuming that you may go only on the segments, and that you may move only up or to the right away from point A, how many different routes are there to your friend's house?

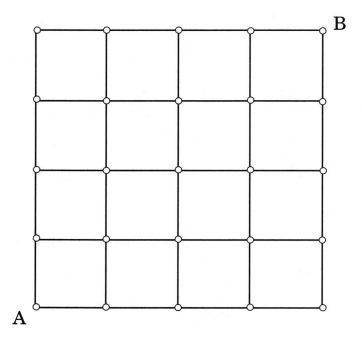

110. What are the next 2 lines?

```
                    4

                  | 4

              |  |  | 4

            3  |  |  4

          2  |  |  3  |  4

        3  |  |  2  |  3  |  4
```

Write an explanation of how you got your answer.

_____

_____

_____

_____

111. The sum of the measures of the interior angles of a triangle (3-gon) is 180 degrees. The sum of the measures of the interior angles of a convex quadrilateral (4-gon) is 360 degrees. The sum of the measures of the interior angles of a convex pentagon (5-gon) is 540 degrees. What is the sum of the measures of the interior angles of a convex polygon with 23 sides (23-gon)?

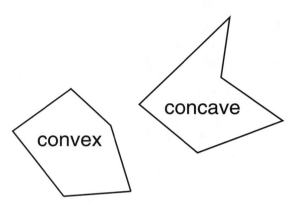

112. You want to save 20% of what you have left after you spend $25 from the $100 you start out with. How much will you save?

113. What are the next three terms of the sequence 1, 2, 3, 2, 1, 2, 3, 4, 2, 1, 2, 3, 4, 3, 2, 3, 4, _____, _____, _____ ?

114. If you got a 40% discount on a $150 pair of sport shoes and 20% off a $200 set of roller blades, what was the percent discount on the total purchase (assuming no taxes are involved)?

Write an explanation of how you got your answer.

_____

_____

_____

115. How many different ways can you paint one cube using only red and blue paint? You can use only one color on a face. Two ways would be considered the same if two cubes painted that way can be rotated so one matches the other exactly, color for color. For example, one way is to paint the cube all red. Another way is to paint the cube all blue. The cube could be painted with four red faces and two blue ones. This could be done more than one way, as could some of the others. Another way is to paint the cube with four blue faces and two red ones. There are more. Give the total number of ways the cube could be painted, including the ones we've already mentioned.

116. What do you call a leg perpendicular to a foot?

117. The number *1961* has rotational symmetry because the number looks the same turned upside down, or rotated *180°*. The assumption is that the upside down *1* still looks like a *1*. Look at the *2, 3, 4, 5, 7* turned upside down. They look different.

$$\textit{Z, S, 4, E, 7}$$

Find the next number after *1961* that has rotational symmetry.

118. What do you get when you cross a rectangle with a rhombus?

119. Can a farmer put 9 ostriches in 4 pens so that there is an odd number of ostriches in each pen and so that each pen has at least one ostrich?

120. The shape of "O" is to the shape of "S" as the shape of what is to the shape of "N"?

Write an explanation of what you did to get your answer.

_____

_____

_____

_____

121. Five teams are playing in a tournament. Each team plays each other team only one time. How many games will be played in all?

122. Why was the right angle in the triangle smiling?

123. What is the next figure in the sequence?

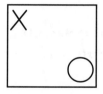 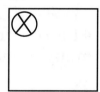 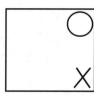 

Write an explanation of how you got your answer.

_____

_____

_____

_____

124. You are given a regular hexagon that has a perimeter of 144 cm. Each side of the regular hexagon has a square attached to it, and the area of each square rests entirely outside of the area defined by the regular hexagon. What is the total area of all of the squares?

125. What do geometry teachers do when they travel?

126.   What African animal do math teachers like best?

127.   The figure below is composed of congruent squares. How many rectangles are in the figure?

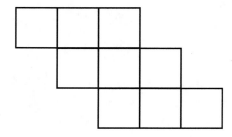

Write an explanation of how you got your answer.

_____

_____

_____

_____

128.   Draw chord AB (not a diameter) in a circle. Draw diameters AC and BD. What kind of polygon will ABCD always be?

Write an explanation of how you got your answer.

_____

_____

_____

_____

FRACTIONS AND DECIMALS

129. After rewriting the following riddle, provide what you think would be a good answer to the question.

The middle $\frac{3}{5}$ of SHOWS,

The first $\frac{1}{3}$ of DOODLE,

The first $\frac{3}{5}$ of YOURS,

The first $\frac{1}{2}$ of KEEPSAKE,

The middle $\frac{1}{5}$ of TRAPS,

The first $\frac{6}{6}$ of TURKEY,

The middle $\frac{1}{2}$ of PINS,

The first $\frac{8}{11}$ of SUSPENSEFUL.

130. How much is 2 times $\frac{1}{2}$ of 498,000?

131. There is a way to show that eight can be half of thirteen. How can that be? You have to think "outside the box" on this one.

132. What percent of the 64 squares on a checkerboard are occupied at the beginning of a game of checkers? Give your answer to the nearest tenth.

133. A class of 30 students has 12 boys. Eight girls have braces and 5 boys have braces. Please answer the following 3 questions.

    1. What is the ratio of boys with braces to boys in the class? $\frac{5}{12}$

    2. What is the ratio of girls with braces to girls in the class? $\frac{8}{18}\frac{4}{9}$

    3. Which group has the larger ratio of students with braces to students in class—boys or girls? _girls_

Write an explanation of how you got the answer to question 3.

_____

_____

_____

_____

134. You are to take a pill every half hour. You have 18 pills to take. How long will the pills last?

135. NOTE TO TEACHER: Read aloud one sentence at a time. Students will compute, then wait for the next sentence.

Take the number of hours in a day. Divide that number by $\frac{1}{2}$ dozen.

Multiply the answer by 2 pairs. Then subtract the number of noses you have. Now add the number of strikes to be "out" in baseball.

136. What fraction of the large square is shaded?

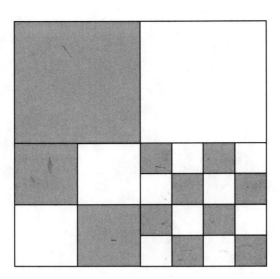

$$\frac{11}{22} = \frac{1}{2}$$

Write an explanation of how you got your answer.

_____

_____

_____

_____

_____

137. From birth, a normal person blinks an average of 25 times a minute when awake. Assume you sleep exactly 8 hours a day and that each year is exactly 365.25 days long. On your next birthday, how many times will you have blinked since your birth? Express your answer to the nearest millionth.

138. You are looking for a 5-digit number where the sum of the ones and tens digits is half of the ten-thousands digit, the thousands digit is half of the ten-thousands digit, and the tens digit is half of the hundreds digit. What is the number?

139. There is a three-volume set of books sitting on a shelf. The front and back covers of the books are each one-eighth inch thick. The page section inside each book is exactly two inches thick. If a cute little bookworm starts eating at page one of volume one and eats along a straight, horizontal path through to the last page of volume three, how far will the cute little fellow travel?

Write an explanation of how you got your answer.

_____

_____

_____

_____

_____

_____

140. A unit fraction has a numerator that is one while the denominator is any counting number other than one. Examples would be

$\frac{1}{2}, \frac{1}{3}, \frac{1}{4}, \frac{1}{5}, \frac{1}{6}, \frac{1}{7}, \frac{1}{13}, \frac{1}{57}, \frac{1}{409}$, etc.

Find 3 different unit fractions that will give a sum that equals one.

141. NOTE TO TEACHER: Read aloud one sentence at a time. Students will compute, then wait for the next sentence.

Take the total number of toes on both feet. Multiply that by the number of babies in twins. Then add the number of months in $\frac{1}{2}$ year.

Subtract the number of thumbs on 2 hands from that answer. Now divide that answer by a dozen.

142. NOTE TO TEACHER: Read aloud one sentence at a time. Students will compute, then wait for the next sentence.

Take the number of sides in a triangle. Multiply that by the number of minutes in an hour. Divide that answer by $\frac{1}{2}$ dozen. Then subtract the number of blackbirds baked in a pie. Finally, add the number of wheels on a bicycle.

143. $\frac{3}{7}$ of what fraction is $\frac{5}{21}$?

144. Suppose you have a staircase made out of cubic blocks. The blocks are stacked so there are no gaps between the faces that should be touching. The bottom layer of the staircase contains 4 cubes, the next layer 3, the next layer 2, and the top step is made up of a single cube. The back of the staircase is made up of 4 cubes all stacked one on top of the other. The bottom of the staircase is also made up of 4 cubes all side by side in one row.

Suppose you are to paint each exposed cube face (except those on the very bottom). If it costs $4.99 for paint and labor to paint a cube face, what will the job cost, rounded to the nearest dollar?

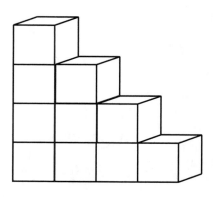

145. Half of your garden is planted in tomatoes. You plant broccoli in a fourth of the ground that is left after the tomatoes are planted. After that, you plant lettuce in half of what is left. The remainder of the garden is planted in cauliflower. What percent of your garden is planted in cauliflower?

146. What three consecutive counting numbers have a sum which is 0.2 of their product? Hint—the largest number is a half-dozen or less.

147. How old would you be in years if you lived 1,000,000 hours? Round your answer to the nearest year.

148. Use each of the following counting numbers exactly once to get an answer of three. You may use any or all of addition, subtraction, multiplication, division, and parentheses as many times as you would like. The numbers may be used in any order. (There is more than one way to do this problem.)

3, 4, 5, 6, 7, 10

149. ACEG is a square. ABMH is a square divided into 9 smaller squares, all of which have the same area. B is the midpoint of AC. D is the midpoint of CE. F is the midpoint of EG. H is the midpoint of AG. J is the midpoint of BC. K is the midpoint of MD. L is the midpoint of DE. N is the midpoint of FE. What part of ACEG is shaded? Express your answer as a fraction or decimal.

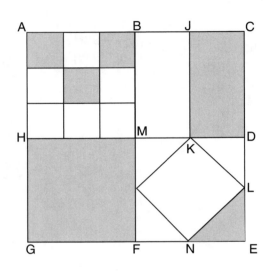

150. Multiply this NUMBER by $1\frac{1}{3}$ or add $1\frac{1}{3}$ to this SAME NUMBER and you will get the same answer. What is the NUMBER?

151. When you roll a pair of dice, one red and one blue, what is the probability they will NOT come up with a sum of three?

Write an explanation of how you got your answer.

_____

_____

_____

_____

152. For the three-digit number ABC, if each of the letters A, B, and C represents a different digit, and A cannot be zero, what is the MINIMUM value of $\dfrac{ABC}{A+B+C}$.

Write an explanation of how you got your answer.

_____

_____

_____

_____

153. The nine volumes of an encyclopedia are numbered 1, 2, 3, 4, 5, 6, 7, 8, and 9. They can be ordered on 2 shelves, one above the other, so they express the fraction one-half as shown:

$$\frac{1}{2} = \frac{6729}{13458}$$ That is, the volumes 6, 7, 2, and 9 would be on the top shelf in that order while the volumes 1, 3, 4, 5, and 8 would be on the bottom shelf in that order. That fraction is equivalent to $\frac{1}{2}$. Arrange the volumes so they are equivalent to $\frac{1}{4}$.

154. If a count of seconds starts on Friday at 3 P.M. and continues nonstop, what day of the week and hour of the day will it be when the 1,000,000th second is reached?

PATTERNS AND PROBLEM SOLVING ————

155. Tell students to write a problem that has the biggest answer they can imagine. They are to work it out and not tell you the answer. When they have finished, you say, "I can write a bigger one!"

156. You are driving a bus that is leaving from Pennsylvania and stopping in New York.

In the beginning, there were 32 passengers on the bus.

At the first bus stop, 11 people got off and 9 people got on.

At the second bus stop, 2 people got off and 2 people got on.

At the third bus stop, 12 people got on and 16 people got off.

At the fourth bus stop, 5 people got on and 3 people got off.

What color are the bus driver's eyes?

Write an explanation of how you got your answer.

_____

_____

_____

_____

157. What kind of horse will stay wherever you put it and never needs to be fed or groomed?

158. What did one math book say to another math book?

159. The farmer has 5 daughters and each one has a brother. How many children does the farmer have?

160. Find the next three letters in this sequence:

F, S, T, F, F, S, S, _T_ , _T_ , _F_

Write an explanation of how you got your answer.

_____

_____

_____

_____

161. Continue the pattern: O T T F F S S _O_ _O_ _T_

Write an explanation of how you got your answer.

_____

_____

_____

_____

162. On the way to town there are 25 trees on the right side of the road. On the way back, traveling on the same road, there are 25 trees on the left side of the road. How many trees are along the road?

163. Which of the 50 U.S. states has the most math teachers?

164. What do you get when a math teacher is a magician?

165. How are these arranged? 8, 5, 4, 9, 1, 7, 6, 2, 0

Write an explanation of how you got your answer.

_____

_____

_____

_____

166. If you take out six letters from the list below, the remaining letters will form a common English word. Find the word.

B S I A N X L E A T N T E A R S

Write an explanation of how you got your answer.

_____

_____

_____

_____

167. Can a man living in Fairbanks, Alaska, be buried in South Carolina?

168. Write a set of numbers on the board and choose a student to be the wizard. *(The teacher secretly gives the wizard a code number, such as 5.)* The wizard leaves the room so that the rest of the class can pick the magic number. The wizard returns to the classroom and answers "yes" or "no" when the teacher points to numbers on the board. The teacher might ask, "Is it 2?" or "Is it 3?" The wizard will know the magic number when the correct number of guesses (such as 5) have been asked. The correct number would be the fifth number asked every time. The class must try to figure out how the wizard knows the magic number.

Variation: The magic number will BE the number that is being pointed to on the board (with no special code number given to the wizard before he leaves the room). For example, write the numbers 1–10 on the board. If a student chooses 4 as the magic number, the wizard will know it when the fourth number pointed to is 4.

When someone has an idea as to HOW it is done, let that student test the theory twice. Don't give the secret away if they don't figure it out. Play it another time.

169.   Why was 6 afraid of 7?

170.   A knight and a bat are thrown into a dungeon together. How will the knight get out?

171.   What is sure to go up, but never goes down?

172. Can you spell just one word with these letters?

UOOSWTDNERJ

173. If you had only a match and entered a room containing an oil lamp, a fireplace, and a gas range, which would you light first?

174. There are 9 stalls in a barn. Each stall holds only 1 horse. If there are 10 horses and only 9 stalls, how can all the horses fit into the 9 stalls without placing more than one horse in each stall?

Explain how you got your answer.

_____

_____

_____

_____

175. A farmer threw 9 ears of corn into the barn. A rat came in and left with 3 ears each day. It took the rat 9 days to take all of the corn. Why?

176. Start with one hand and count backwards from 10, pointing to each finger and thumb one time. Add that number to the five fingers on the other hand. How many fingers do you have?

177. Mo said, "I saw the most peculiar pine tree today! Every part of that tree involved the number 3! There were 3 main trunks, 3 main limbs, 3 smaller branches on each limb, and on each of those there were 3 birds and 3 acorns! Mo quickly calculated and told his friend Jo the total number of acorns. Can you?

178. When you cross out exactly seven letters in the grid shown, you will reveal two and only two numbers. What are the two numbers?

S	N	E	F	V
E	T	N	O	L
E	E	T	I	R
E	R	N	U	S

179. There are exactly 11 people in a room, and each person shakes hands with every other person in the room. When person A shakes with person B, B is also shaking with A. That counts as ONE handshake. How many handshakes will there be when everyone is finished shaking hands with everyone else?

180. Observe the four straight line segments below. Add 5 more straight
line segments to make 10.

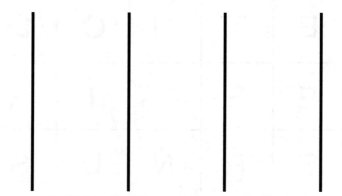

SOLUTIONS

1. Between 1 and 100, there are 19 numbers having a nine, including the number 9. (9, 19, 29, 39, 49, 59, 69, 79, 89, 90, 91, 92, 93, 94, 95, 96, 97, 98, 99)

2. Varies. (For example, 6 becomes 9, 69 becomes 96, 106 becomes 109.)

   Note: "Turning upside down" in this format has the digits staying in the same place value position. Some students might think in terms of rotating a number 180°, which would make 106 become 901. Such divergent thinking should be encouraged.

3. 5

   Note: Draw a picture, or have students act out being the cars.

4. A dime and a nickel. One coin is not a dime, but the other one is!

5. Varies.

6. You would have the 5 coins you took. (Some would say that you have 17 coins, assuming the piggy bank belongs to you.)

7. The new ten dollar bill. A ten dollar bill is worth more than a one dollar bill.

8. One thousand. Remember 101 is one hundred one, not one hundred and one! An additional solution and conceivably the correct answer is "naught." Naught is defined as nothing. One of the definitions of nothing is zero. (Neufeldt, Victoria, Editor in Chief, Webster's New World College Dictionary, Third Edition, 1996. Macmillan, NY)

9. There are 13 ways to pay 25 cents

   25 pennies
   20 pennies, 1 nickel
   15 pennies, 2 nickels
   15 pennies, 1 dime
   10 pennies, 3 nickels
   10 pennies, 1 nickel, 1 dime
   5 pennies, 4 nickels
   5 pennies, 2 nickels, 1 dime
   5 pennies, 2 dimes
   5 nickels
   3 nickels, 1 dime

   1 nickel, 2 dimes
   1 quarter

   Note: This could become a decimal problem if the coin values were so written.

   Rubric: 3 possible points

   1 point (content): Conclude there are 13 ways to pay 25 cents

   1 point (content): Correctly list the number of ways to pay 25 cents

   1 point (clarity): The explanation is clearly written

10. th, th. The st comes from 1st, nd comes from 2nd, rd comes from 3rd, and th comes from 4th. Therefore 5th and 6th would come next and the additions to the sequence would be th and th.

11. e, t. two, four, six, eight, ten, twelve, fourteen, sixteen, <u>eighteen</u>, <u>twenty</u>. The letters stand for the first letters of the number words when counting by 2s from two to twenty.

12. Digits for house numbers. Typical guesses include nuts, bolts, nails, washers, etc. Actually the 1 is made up of one digit, 50 is made up of 2 digits, and 200 is made up of 3 digits. If 1, 50, and 200 are thought of as house numbers, digits for a house number are being purchased at a dollar each.

13. $47. The profit was $47. The sellers' names were Forty and Jonesy.

    Note: Many students groan at questions like this, but they do get the point. More significantly, they frequently ask the question of others, which can stimulate some positive conversations about the study of mathematics.

14. 0 appears 12 times. 1 appears 21 times. Each of the digits 2–9 appear 20 times each. Zero appears 11 times in the units place and 1 time in the tens place. One appears ten times in the units place, ten times in the tens place and one time in the hundreds place. Each of the other digits appears ten times in the units place and ten times in the tens place.

Rubric: 4 possible points

1 point (content): Give the correct number of times 0 appears

1 point (content): Give the correct number of times 1 appears

1 point (content): Give the correct number of times each digit 2–9 appears

1 point (clarity): The explanation is clearly written

15. 217. Consider the whole numbers from 200 to 299 inclusive. There are 19 numbers in that set which contain a 3 (203, 213, 223, 230, 231, 232, 233, 234, 235, 236, 237, 238, 239, 243, 253, 263, 273, 283, and 293). That means 81 numbers between 200 and 300 inclusive do not contain a 3.

No whole numbers from 300 to 399 would work since they all contain a 3.

Consider the numbers from 400 to 499, inclusive. There are 19 numbers that contain at least one 2 (402, 412, 420, 421, 422, 423, 424, 425, 426, 427, 428, 429, 432, 442, 452, 462, 472, 482, and 492). However, two of the numbers in that set contain a 3 (423 and 432) and must be eliminated, leaving 17 numbers containing at least one 2.

The other seven sets of numbers (0–99, 100–199, 400–499, 600–699, 700–799, 800–899, and 900–999) also each contain 17 numbers with at least one 2 in them.

Therefore, 81 + 0 + (8 x 17) = 217

Rubric: 5 possible points

1 point (content): Eliminate all values from 300 to 399 inclusive

1 point (content): Realize that only 19 values from 200 to 299 inclusive would be eliminated

1 point (content): Correct arithmetic

1 point (content): Realize that 17 values for each of the other groups of numbers would meet the criteria

1 point (clarity): The explanation is clearly written

16. two sows 'n bucks (two thousand bucks)

Note: Many students groan at questions like this, but they do get the point. More significantly, they frequently ask the question of others, which can stimulate some positive conversations about the study of mathematics.

17. One. Everyone has one *birth day,* but different *anniversaries* of that day.

18. 11 of each. 11($0.25) + 11($0.10) + 11($0.05) = $2.75 + $1.10 + $0.55 = $4.40

Guess and Check is most likely response.

OR

Divide $4.40 by (0.25 + 0.1 + 0.05) and get 11, which means 11 of each coin.

Rubric: 3 possible points

1 point (content): Recognize the need to divide by $0.40 since there is the same number of each coin

1 point (content): Correct arithmetic

1 point (clarity): The explanation is clearly written

19. The value of one coin must be multiplied by an even number. The value of the other coin must be multiplied by an odd number. If the student tells you an even answer, the right hand holds the penny. If the student tells you an odd number, the right hand holds the dime.

Left Hand: **dime** Right Hand: **penny**

$ 0.50 + $ 0.08 = $ 0.58

Left Hand: **penny** Right Hand: **dime**

$ 0.05 + $ 0.80 = $ 0.85

Rubric: 3 possible points

1 point (content): Logic for determining the solution is correct

1 point (content): Correct arithmetic

1 point (clarity): The explanation is clearly written

20. One half-dollar, one quarter, and four dimes. To make change for a nickel, you would need pennies. You would need five pennies (or a multiple of 5) since your total is $1.15. Since you have only six coins and there is no coin worth $1.10, you cannot have any pennies.

Since you cannot change a dime, you cannot have 2 nickels (perhaps you have one).

Since you cannot change a quarter and you have no pennies, you cannot have 3 nickels or 5 nickels.

Since you cannot change a half-dollar, you cannot have 2 quarters or a quarter and change for a quarter. You could have 2 dimes and a quarter as long as there are not 5 pennies or any nickels. You could have 4 dimes and still not be able to change a quarter or half-dollar.

21. There are 50 ways to pay 50 cents.

50 pennies
45 pennies, 1 nickel
40 pennies, 2 nickels
40 pennies, 1 dime
35 pennies, 3 nickels,
35 pennies, 1 nickels, 1 dime
30 pennies, 4 nickels
30 pennies, 2 nickels, 1 dime
30 pennies, 2 dimes
25 pennies, 5 nickels
25 pennies, 3 nickels, 1 dime
25 pennies, 1 nickels, 2 dimes
25 pennies, 1 quarter
20 pennies, 6 nickels
20 pennies, 4 nickels, 1 dime
20 pennies, 2 nickels, 2 dimes
20 pennies, 3 dimes
20 pennies, 1 nickel, 1 quarter
15 pennies, 7 nickels
15 pennies, 5 nickels, 1 dime
15 pennies, 3 nickels, 2 dimes
15 pennies, 1 nickel, 3 dimes
15 pennies, 1 dime, 1 quarter
10 pennies, 8 nickels
10 pennies, 6 nickels, 1 dime
10 pennies, 4 nickels, 2 dimes
10 pennies, 2 nickels, 3 dimes
10 pennies, 4 dimes
10 pennies, 3 nickels, 1 quarter
10 pennies, 1 nickel, 1 dime, 1 quarter
5 pennies, 9 nickels,
5 pennies, 7 nickels, 1 dime
5 pennies, 5 nickels, 2 dimes

5 pennies, 3 nickels, 3 dimes
5 pennies, 1 nickel, 4 dimes
5 pennies, 4 nickels, 1 quarter
10 nickels
5 pennies, 2 nickels, 1 dime, 1 quarter
5 pennies, 2 dimes, 1 quarter
8 nickels, 1 dime
6 nickels, 2 dimes
4 nickels, 3 dimes
2 nickels, 4 dimes
5 nickels, 1 quarter
3 nickels, 1 dime, 1 quarter
1 nickel, 2 dimes, 1 quarter
5 nickels, 1 quarter
5 dimes
2 quarters
1 half-dollar

Note: This could become a decimal problem if the coin values were so written.

22. Varies.

Note: Scoring could be altered to allow other team members to provide the correct sum if a player missed it.

Students could add the same number and possibly win with little difficulty. The realization that adding the same number is a very fast way to accomplish the task is an important idea. You might want to reward their creativity and thoughtfulness in some way and then alter the rules so that using the same number is not permitted.

23. 2. If they had 10 and ate *all but two* of them, then there are two left. $10 - 8 = 2$

24. 60.

x = number

x + 10

2x + 20

2x + 120

x + 60

x − x + 60

25. 7, 1, 1, 1, 1, 1, 1. Many students will assume that the numbers being used must be different

26. 5. This is really the addition problem

```
  53789
+ 26415
  80204
```

27. Pages 11, 49, and 50 will also be missing. Look at any section of a newspaper. Page 2 is on the back of page 1. Pages 1 and 2 are attached to the last 2 pages of the section (in this case, pages 59 and 60).

1, 2 are attached to 59, 60

3, 4 are attached to 57, 58

5, 6 are attached to 55, 56

7, 8 are attached to 53, 54

9, 10 are attached to 51, 52

11, 12 are attached to 49, 50

Rubric: 3 possible points

1 point (content): Recognize that 1 and 2 are connected with 59 and 60

1 point (content): Recognize that 11 and 12 are connected with 49 and 50

1 point (clarity): The explanation is clearly written

28. 5

Fill the 4 from the 10. (6 in 10, 4 in 4)

Fill the 3 from the 4. (3 in 3, 1 in 4)

Pour the rest of the 3 back into the 10. (0 in 3, 9 in 10)

Pour the rest of the 4 into the 3. (1 in 3)

Refill the 4 from the 10. (5 in 10, 4 in 4)

Rubric: 2 possible points

1 point (content): Recognize the shortest pattern

1 point (content): Correct arithmetic

1 point (clarity): The explanation is clearly written

29. 2. Drive 7000 miles and trade off the two front tires. Drive 7000 more miles. Take the two that used to be on the front and put them on the back (the back ones have 14,000 miles on them and are worn out). Now go the remaining 7000 miles.

Rubric: 3 possible points

1 point (content): Recognize the pattern of taking off tires 2 at a time

1 point (content): Realize that one pair of tires can go 14,000 before removal

1 point (clarity): The explanation is clearly written

30. 1 + 333 + 777 = 1111. Remove two 1s and three 9s. The students should realize that the clue is in the 7s and 3s since that sum ends in zero. A similar approach could be used with 9s and 1s but quickly gets to the point that another 1 is needed but not available.

31. 8 pigs and 9 ducks. Students may draw pictures (diagrams), guess and test, or use formulas to solve.

P = pigs D = ducks

$P + D = 17$

$P = 17 - D$

$4P + 2D = 50$ because pigs have 4 feet and ducks have 2 feet.

$4(17 - D) + 2D = 50$

$68 - 4D + 2D = 50$

$68 - 2D = 50$

$-2D = -18$

$D = 9$

$P = 17 - D$

$P = 17 - 9$

$9 = 17 - D$

$D = 8$

Note: Your students will probably not use the algebraic approach to solve this problem because they do not have those skills. However, the thought process involved is the same, even without the variable. Doing problems like this is a critical first step toward developing those necessary algebra skills.

32. Varies. Divide the sum by 3. The result will be the center date. Subtract 7 from the result to get the first date, and add 7 to the result to get the third date.

This is a good example of a multistep problem that students need to become efficient at solving.

Challenging the students to figure out how you are doing this problem will develop their problem-solving skills.

33. 134. (5 x 5) + 9 + 100 = 134

34. Varies. Divide the sum by 3 and the result will always be the *center date!* If X is the center date, the three dates are X – 1, X, and X + 1. Adding the three dates gives a sum of 3X. Subtract 1 *to find the first date.* Add 1 *to find the last date.*

35. Varies. Divide the sum by 4. Ignore any remainder. The answer is the second date in the list. Let the first date selected be X. Then the next 3 dates are X + 1, X + 2, and X + 3. Adding all four dates you get 4X + 6. Dividing that sum by 4 will always give you X + 1 with a remainder of 2. Ignoring the remainder, the day is X + 1 and if X is the first day, then X + 1 is the second day.

Note: Your students will probably not use the algebraic approach to solve this problem because they do not have those skills. However, the thought process involved is the same, even without the variable. Doing problems like this is a critical first step toward developing those necessary algebra skills.

This is also a good example of a multistep problem that students need to become efficient at solving.

Challenging the students to figure out how you are doing this problem will develop their problem-solving skills.

36. The dog weighs 9 pounds and the cat 18 pounds. The problem does not state the dog is male. The cat is the boy and the dog is the girl. Algebraically you would say:

Let X = the lighter weight animal

2X = the heavier weight animal

X + 2X = 27

3X = 27

X = 9, the weight of the lighter animal

2X = 18, the weight of the heavier animal

Since the dog is the odd weight, the dog must weigh 9 pounds.

Since he weighs twice as much as she does, the cat must be the 18-pounder.

Note: Your students will probably not set up the problem to be done algebraically as shown here. However, they will probably use this line of reasoning to get to their answer. It is important that you encourage this type thinking as formative work for the algebra which is in their future.

A further value to this problem lies in the multistep process required to solve it.

37. The sum of the digits in each row, column, and diagonal is 36!

A missing figure can be found by adding the digits that remain in a row, column, or diagonal and subtracting the sum from 36. The difference is the missing digit.

Note: This takes some practice. The time is worth it, particularly if you encourage the students to try to determine how you are doing the problem.

38. 25. This is an application of 1 + 3 + 5 + 7 +.... Since the total is known, there are two ways to arrive at the number of groups. One is to keep adding the odd numbers until 625 is reached. The other is to realize that 1 + 3 = 4, 1 + 3 + 5 = 9, 1 + 3 + 5 + 7 = 16, etc. So each new group raises the total to the next consecutive square number ($1^2, 2^2, 3^2, 4^2$, etc.) so you need to find only the square root of 625 to get 25.

39. 9. Using 9 for C, A + C = 10. 10 + B is the expanded form of 1B (remember, A = 1).

OR

AB means 10A + B which equals A + B + C.

10A + B = A + B + C

9A = C (subtracting A + B from both sides of the equation)

B can be any digit; A must be 1 (If A = 0, you violate conditions of the problem.)

If A = 1, then C = 9.

OR

When C = 9

A + B + C = AB

  1 + 1 + 9 = 11

  1 + 2 + 9 = 12

  1 + 3 + 9 = 13

  1 + 4 + 9 = 14

  1 + 5 + 9 = 15

  1 + 6 + 9 = 16

  1 + 7 + 9 = 17

  1 + 8 + 9 = 18

  1 + 9 + 9 = 19

No other value for C will do this.

Note: The explanation to this problem is complex. Students need to encounter this type of situation as soon as is reasonable in their experiences to develop their problem-solving and number skills.

40. 45. (Method will vary—calculator/paper and pencil). The easy way is to know that the sum of the first n consecutive counting numbers (from Gauss) is $\frac{n(n + 1)}{2}$. Knowing that, solve for the first one that gives a sum greater than or equal to 1,000.

This problem could also be done on a calculator. Enter 1 + 2 + 3 + 4 + 5 + ... until the sum equals or exceeds 1000.

This could also be done with pencil and paper in a manner similar to the one used for the calculator.

Rubric: 3 possible points

1 point (content): Recognize the pattern of adding successive counting numbers

1 point (content): Correct arithmetic

1 point (clarity): The explanation is clearly written

41. 119. The two-digit multiples of 7 are 14, 21, 28, 35, 42, 49, 56, 63, 70, 77, 84, 91, and 98. Two multiples, 28 and 91, have digits that add to 10. 28 + 91 = 119.

Rubric: 4 possible points

1 point (content): Know the multiples of 7

1 point (content): Know which multiples of 7 to select

1 point (content): Correct arithmetic

1 point (clarity): The explanation is clearly written

42. 16. The sum of the numbers in each of the triangles is 58.

43. A = 1, B = 4, and C = 8. A cannot be greater than 3 since 4 or greater would require the sum to be a four-digit number. By process of elimination:

If C = 0 then B = 0 and that is not allowed.

If C = 1 then B = 3 and the tens column would not correctly sum.

If C = 2 then B = 6 and the tens column would not correctly sum.

If C = 3 then B = 9 and the tens column would not correctly sum.

If C = 4 then B = 2 and the tens column would not correctly sum.

If C = 5 then B = 5 and that is not allowed.

If C = 6 then B = 8 and the tens column would not correctly sum.

If C = 7 then B = 1 and the tens column would not correctly sum.

If C = 8 then B = 4, which works.

If C = 9 then B = 7 and the tens column would not correctly sum.

With C = 8 and B = 4, then A = 1.

Note: The logic required for the solution to this problem is complex and many students will struggle with it. However, it is a good problem to assign because those who can think through it will be the potential mathematical stars of the future.

Rubric: 3 possible points

1 point (content): Realize that A must be less than 4 to avoid a 4-digit sum

1 point (content): Recognize the impact of incorrect selections on the sum

1 point (clarity): The explanation is clearly written.

44.

6	10	1	8
	4	9	7
		5	2
			3

Note: There are other arrangements that will work.

Guess and check.

45. Accept one or all of the following:

The ones digit in the sum is one less than the digit added to 9.

The sum of digits in each product is 9.

In each column of the products, 1 through 9 appears.

46. 91, 117, 119, 143, 153, 169, 171, 187

91 = 7 x 13, 117 = 9 x 13, 119 = 7 x 17, 143 = 11 x 13, 153 = 9 x 17, 169 = 13 x 13, 171 = 9 x 19, 187 = 11 x 17.

47. Tell the students the answer is 12. The teacher will know the final number because of the following:

X	the number	4	17
3X	triple it	12	51
3X + 36	add 36	48	87
X + 12	divide by 3	16	29
12	subtract original number	12	12

Note: The instructions for this problem can be altered. For example, rather than subtracting the original number in the last step, have the students subtract 12. Then their answer will be their original number. You could also double the original number, then add some value, divide by 2, and subtract the original number to have each student end up with the same answer. Similar other variations can be developed. The solution is easiest to see if you do the problem using algebra first.

48. 7

$3N + 6 = N + 20$

(where N is the number)

$2N = 14$

$N = 7$

This can also be done with guess and check.

Note: Your students will probably not use as sophisticated an algebraic presentation as shown here. However, it is possible that they will have the formative stages present in their thinking process.

49. 75 pounds. The weight shifted, but it is still the same weight on the scale.

Note: Get a scale and have the students weigh with both feet on the scale and then again with one foot on the scale. Some scales will give a different value when the student is standing on one foot unless they place their foot close to the center of the scale.

Rubric: 2 points

1 point (content): Realize that the weight does not change

1 point (clarity): Explanation is clearly written

50. 10. $\{ (2 \times 4) \div 1 \} + 2 = 10$

51. $1234567 \times 8 + 7 = 9876543$

$12345678 \times 8 + 8 = 98765432$

$123456789 \times 8 + 9 = 987654321$

52. $1.50

OR $0.75

7 pieces means 6 cuts. $6(\$0.25) = \$1.50$

OR

Cut one piece into two parts. Place one piece on top of the other and make a second cut, giving 4 pieces. Stack 3 of those 4 pieces and make a third cut, giving a total of 7 pieces, including the 1 that had not been cut the last time.

Rubric: 3 possible points

1 point (content]: Recognize the value of stacking parts and then cutting

OR 1 point (content): Recognize that the total number of cuts is 6 (without stacking)

1 point (content): Correct arithmetic

1 point (clarity): The explanation is clearly written

Note: This rubric shows a total value of 3 because it is unlikely that a student would do the problem two different ways. If, however, a student did the problem two different ways, bonus points would be advisable. That student would be showing powerful problem-solving potential and flexible thinking.

53. 496. 1, 2, 4, 8, 16, 31, 62, 124, 248, 496.

Note: The number of known perfect numbers is not that large and their investigation leads into interesting areas of number theory and the history of mathematics.

54.

55. 153. For example, if you start with 12, you will get

$$1^3 + 2^3 = 9$$

$$9^3 = 729$$

$$7^3 + 2^3 + 9^3 = 1080$$

$$1^3 + 0^3 + 8^3 + 0^3 = 513$$

Finally, $5^3 + 1^3 + 3^3 = 153$

Note: The number of steps required to get to 153 will vary with the number selected initially.

56. Maria has traveled 6 times as far as Manuel. Going from the first floor to the second floor is one elevator move. Going from the second to the third floor is a second elevator move. Going from the third to the fourth floor is a third elevator move. Going from the fourth floor to the fifth is a fourth elevator move. So, going from the first to the fifth floor takes 4 elevator moves. Similarly, there would be 24 elevator moves going from the first to the

25th floor. $\frac{24}{4} = 6$

Rubric: 4 possible points

1 point (content): Recognize 4 elevator moves from the first to fifth floor

1 point (content): Recognize 24 elevator moves from the first to 25th floor

1 point (content): Correct arithmetic

1 point (clarity): The explanation is clearly written

57. 9. $(12 + 36 - 12) \div 4 = 9$

58. 58. $[(16 \div 4) \times 12] + 10 = 58$

59. Multi-ply tires.

Note: Many students groan at riddles like this, but they do get the point. More significantly, they frequently ask the riddle of others, which can stimulate some positive conversations about the study of mathematics.

60. Each of them has a vertical line segment as the left part of the letter.

61. 3, 5, 7. Since the product ends in 5, one of the factors must be 5. Now the known addends are 1, 5, and 9, which add to 15. The remaining two addends must sum to 10. 1 x 5 x 9 = 45. Since 945 ÷ 45 = 21, their product must be 21, __ x __ = 21. The factors of 21 that give a sum of 10 are 3 and 7.

62. (A, B, C, D) = (12, 2, 3, 16). Given A x B, A & B could be 1, 24; 2, 12; 3, 8; or 4, 6.

But A + B = 14, so A and B have to be 2 & 12.

B x C = 6 and B has to be 2 or 12. Since all numbers are counting numbers, B must be 2, C is 3, and A is 12.

A x D = 192, so D = 16 since A =12 and $\frac{192}{12}$ = 16

63. 26. Guess and check

OR

List the set of answers for 2 extra and 5 extra and find the matching value that is the smallest over 10.

Two extra—14, 18, 22, 26, 30, 34, 38,…4N + 2 (N is a counting number)

One extra—11, 16, 21, 26, 31, 36, …5N + 1

OR

Divide 6 by 4 and get a remainder of 2. The next number that, when divided by 4, gives a remainder of 2 will be 4 greater than 6, or 10. The next one after that will be 4 greater than 10, or 14. Then 18. Then 22. Then 26. Then 30, etc.

Divide 6 by 5 and get a remainder of 1. Continue in a manner similar to the one described for 4 and you will get 26 as the first common number.

Note: Your students will probably not use the algebraic approach to solve this problem because they do not have those skills. However, the thought process involved is the same, even without the variable. Doing problems like this is a critical first step toward developing those necessary algebra skills.

This is also a good example of a multistep problem that students need to become efficient at solving.

64. If it is dropped from a height greater than 5 feet, it will fall 5 feet without breaking, but after that, it'll probably break when it lands.

Note: Many students groan at questions like this, but they do get the point. More significantly, they frequently ask the question of others, which can stimulate some positive conversations about the study of mathematics.

65. 12. A dozen is 12, no matter what the items.

66. At deci-malls

Note: Many students groan at riddles like this, but they do get the point. More significantly, they frequently ask the riddle of others, which can stimulate some positive conversations about the study of mathematics.

67. 0.75 minutes = 1 hour 15 minutes. The shoes have nothing to do with it. The times are equal.

68. 8 minutes. A picture helps. Fifteen miles per hour means the train goes 1 mile in 4 minutes. At the end of the first 4 minutes, the train is completely in the tunnel. It takes another 4 minutes for the caboose to get out the other end.

Rubric: 3 possible points

1 point (content): Recognize that 15 m.p.h. means 1 mile in 4 minutes

1 point (content): Recognize that there is a need for two 4-minute segments

1 point (clarity): The explanation is clearly written

69. 1 hour. 8:00 P.M. to 9:00 P.M. = 1 hour

8:00 A.M. to 9:00 A.M. = 1 hour

Note: Time-savvy students may argue that they have a digital alarm clock that uses both AM and PM setting options. This would be a wonderful opportunity to discuss the differences between analog and digital clocks, and the advantages and disadvantages of each.

70. 3 feet. OR, It depends upon how many people are standing in the yard!

Note: Many students groan at questions like this, but they do get the point. More significantly, they frequently ask the question of others, which can stimulate some positive conversations about the study of mathematics.

71. Take 1 nugget from the first bag, 2 from the second, and 3 from the third. A total weight of 6.1 means the real gold is in the first bag; 6.2 means the real gold is in the second bag; 6.3 means the real gold is in the third bag.

Rubric: 3 possible points

1 point (content): Recognize need to use one nugget from each of the 3 bags

1 point (content): Recognize need to use a nugget from each bag

1 point (content): Correct arithmetic

1 point (clarity): The explanation is clearly written

72. 1 hour. Rover gets one pill right away, one 30 minutes after that, and the last pill 30 minutes after that.

Rubric: 3 possible points

1 point (content): Recognize pattern of using beginning and end time both

1 point (content): Recognize pattern of adding a half-hour for each pill taken

1 point (clarity): The explanation is clearly written

73. Holes. Put holes in the barrel. That way, you have removed some of the material (matter) and it weighs less.

Students may try this as an experiment with any object (i.e., cardboard, paper, clay).

74. 150 square units. Consider the top front right cube. 3 faces of that cube are exposed (shaded) and the other 3 faces are not exposed so they would not contribute to the surface area computation. Removing that cube would remove those 3 faces from the total but it would introduce 3 new faces to the situation. Thus, there is no change in the surface area. Ditto for the other 7 corner cubes. So the surface area is (5 x 5) for each face, times 6 faces, or 5 x 5 x 6 = 150.

OR

Each face of the big cube has 25 square units originally so the total surface area is 150 square units. Four squares are removed from each face, leaving 150 − (6 x 4) = 150 − 24 = 126. But, the cavity in each of the 8 corners adds 3 unit squares back in so you have to add 8 x 3 = 24 to the 126, giving 150.

Rubric: 3 possible points

1 point (content): Recognize the pattern

1 point (content): Correct arithmetic

1 point (clarity): The explanation is clearly written

75. Take me to your liter.

Note: Many students groan at riddles like this, but they do get the point. More significantly, they frequently ask the riddle of others, which can stimulate some positive conversations about the study of mathematics.

76. One more inch and it would be a foot!

Note: Many students groan at questions like this, but they do get the point. More significantly, they frequently ask the question of others, which can stimulate some positive conversations about the study of mathematics.

77. At about 7:06. Model the answer with a geared demonstration clock or an alarm clock.

78. 13 hours. 8:00 P.M. to 9:00 P.M. = 1 hour

9:00 P.M. to 9:00 A.M. = 12 hours

1 + 12 = 13

79. 11. The bell chimes 6 times in the first five seconds because the first chime starts the timing at zero seconds. The second chime happens at the end of the first second. The third chime happens at the end of the second second. The fourth chime happens at the end of the third second. The fifth chime happens at the end of the fourth second. The sixth chime happens at the end of the fifth second. Continuing that pattern, the eleventh chime will happen at the end of the tenth second.

A rule could be "Number of chimes = second number + 1." The advantage of this rule is the background it creates for algebra.

Rubric: 3 possible points:

1 point (content): Recognize the timing starts with the first chime

1 point (content): State a rule

1 point (clarity): The explanation is clearly written

80. M. There is 1 M in the words "every minute," 1 M in the words "each month," two Ms in the words "next millennium," and 1 M in "a million years." Some students may try to claim N as a solution. This would be possible if you were looking only at the words minute, month, millennium, and million. However, N does not work as defined above since there are 3 Ns in "next millennium."

Rubric: 2 possible points

1 point (content): Recognize the pattern

1 point (clarity): The explanation is clearly written

Note: This explanation could be very short. It is important that students have the opportunity to search for the "unusual" patterns. This promotes flexibility of thought, which is critical in upper-level mathematics.

81. 12. Each month has at least 28 days, even though some have more.

82. 310 cm. Project all vertical and horizontal segments of the steps to the most outer parallel segment on its respective side or top (not to the bottom). You then have a rectangle that is 128 by 27. Doubling both of those gives 310 cm.

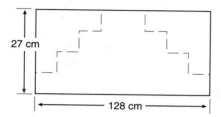

83. Between 5:30 and 5:45 P.M.

4:00 P.M. has 1 person.

By 4:15 P.M., 3 people know (1 + 2 = 3).

By 4:30 P.M., 7 people know (3 + 4 = 7—the 2 new people who were called each tell 2, giving a total of 4 to be added to the old sum of 3).

By 4:45 P.M., 15 people know (7 + 8 = 15—the 4 new people each tell 2, giving a total of 8 to be added to the old sum of 7).

And so the pattern continues:

5:00 P.M. has 15 + 16 (8 newly called people tell 16 more people).

5:15 P.M. has 31 + 32 (16 newly called people tell 32 more people).

5:30 P.M. has 63 + 64 = 127 (32 newly called people tell 64 more people).

5:45 P.M. has 127 + 128 (64 newly called people tell 128 more people).

Somewhere between 5:30 P.M. and 5:45 P.M., 200 people will know the name of the winner.

84. 88,440,293 seconds
Subtracting:

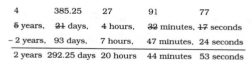

2 years x 365.25days/yr x 24 hr/dy x 60 min/hr x 60 sec/min +

292.25 days x 24 hr/dy x 60 min/hr x 60 sec/min +

20 hr x 60 min/hr x 60 sec/min +

44 min x 60 sec/min +

53 seconds =

63,115,200 + 25,250,400 + 72,000 + 2,640 + 53 = 88,440,293 seconds

Rubric: 2 possible points

1 point (content): Conversions set up correctly

1 point (content): Correct arithmetic

85. The child was born before July 4, 1776.

Note: Some responses could be extremely creative. For example, the child was born in an airplane over the Boston airport.

86. 10. You would pass the first train 15 minutes into your trip (it is due in 15 minutes at A, from where you just left). After that, you will pass a train about each half hour for another 4.5 hours. That means you pass a total of 10 trains.

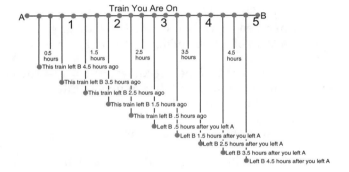

Train You Are On

Note: It will help students if they establish a model of this problem.

Rubric: 4 possible points

1 point (content): Realize the first train is seen 15 minutes after departing

1 point (content): Realize a train is seen every half hour after the first train

1 point (content): Correct arithmetic

1 point (clarity): The explanation is clearly written

87. 68 years old. There was no year zero. The 2 years that are subtracted are one for year zero, and one for not yet making it to the birthday in year A.D. 3.

Note: Try a smaller problem, such as if he were born on March 10, 4 B.C. and died on March 9, A.D. 3. Then he turned one on 3/10/3 B.C., two on 3/10/2 B.C., three on 3/10/1 B.C.,

four on A.D. 3/10/1. (There was no year 0), five on A.D. 3/10/2, yet never lived to A.D. 3/10/3; therefore, he would have been 5 years old, which is the B.C. year (4) + the A.D. year (3) − 2 = 5 years old.

Rubric: 3 possible points

1 point (content): Realize there was no year zero

1 point (content): Realize the impact of not reaching the birthday

1 point (clarity): The explanation is clearly written

88. 34. There is one such reading between 11 and 12 (11:22), 1 and 2 (1:22), 3 and 4 (3:22), and 4 (4:22) and 5.

There are 15 such readings between each of 12 and 1 and 2 and 3. 12:2X accounts for 10 of them (12:20, 12:21, 12:22, 12:23, 12:24, 12:25, 12:26, 12:27, 12:28, and 12:29) as well as 12:02, 12:12, 12:32, 12:42, and 12:52. The same applies between 2 and 3 (2:20, 2:21, 2:22, 2:23, 2:24, 2:25, 2:26, 2:27, 2:28, 2:29, as well as 2:02, 2:12, 2:32, 2:42, and 2:52).

89. Insert the line segment over the "1" of the "10" making "15 to 5," which in time telling, is the same as 4:45.

90. The next odd date is 1-1-3111 and the last even date was 8-28-888. This problem requires guess and check, coupled with logic. The student should conclude that the first move would be to look for an even or odd year. To get the next odd date after November 19, 1999, you must go outside any date that begins with a 2, which eliminates everything from 2000 through 2999 inclusive. That is, one must go into something beyond the 31st century. Thus, the year has to be 31?? where all the digits are odd. The first candidate is 3111. Now shift to the months and the first odd month is January (1). The first odd day is the first day (1). Thus, the date is 1-1-3111.

For the last even year before February 2, 2000, you must go below 900 since all of the dates in the 10th through the 20th centuries inclusive have an odd digit. Similarly, all of the 890 dates must be eliminated as is the case with 889. So 888 is the first even year in the category we are looking for. The last even months of 10 and 12 will not work because they have odd digits. That means the month must be 8. The last totally even day must be 28, so the object of the search is 8-28-888.

91. 5. You pass the one that left A at 8:00 at the B station as you leave at 10:00. A quarter of the way into your trip, you will pass the bus that left A at 9:00. Halfway along, you would pass the bus that left A the same time you left B. Three-quarters of the way along, you would pass the bus that left A at 11:00. You will pass the fifth bus as it leaves A while you pull in.

Rubric: 3 possible points

1 point (content): Recognize time intervals when another bus is seen

1 point (content): Operations with times are correct

1 point (clarity): The explanation is clearly written

Note: The solution arbitrarily uses a 10:00 departure for the bus from Station B. The trip for any bus takes 2 hours. The departure time could have been any hour. The key is that, as they are leaving the station, people on the departing bus will see the bus that left 2 hours ago, the bus that left 1 hour ago, the bus that left the same time they did, the bus that left an hour after they did, and the fifth and final bus, which will leave as they pull into station A.

92. Y. First letter of standard units for telling time (Second, Minute, Hour, Day, Week, Month, Year).

93. 19, 8. The odd-numbered terms in the sequence (first, third, fifth—9, 11, 13, 15, 17) are increasing odd counting numbers, going up to the next odd counting number on each step. The even-numbered terms (second, fourth, sixth—18, 16, 14, 12, 10) are decreasing even counting numbers, going down to the next even counting number on each step.

Rubric: 4 possible points

1 point (content): Recognize the odd terms as increasing odd counting numbers

1 point (content): Recognize the even terms as decreasing even counting numbers

1 point (content): Recognize the integrated patterns

1 point (clarity): The explanation is clearly written

94. 8, 1. On a clock face, start at 2 and move five hours in a clockwise direction every time.

Rubric: 3 possible points

1 point (content): Recognition of the need to use a clock face

1 point (content): Apply the pattern correctly

1 point (clarity): The explanation is clearly written

95. S, O, N. They are the first letters of the months of the year: September, October, November.

Rubric: 2 possible points

1 point (content): Recognition of the pattern

1 point (clarity): The explanation is clearly written

Note: It is important to ask students this type of question. It helps them learn to think in different ways. This type of question also stimulates discussions about mathematics and patterning as they try to stump others with the pattern.

96. 8. The sum of the first and last numbers is 17. The sum of the second and second to last numbers is 17, and so on so that $9 + c = 17$.

97. 21, 22. This is a list of counting numbers beginning with the letter "T." They are arranged in increasing order. Also acceptable: 22, 23, (30). Ten can be added to each number in the first set of three to find the next number in the next set of three.

Rubric: 2 possible points

1 point (content): Recognition of pattern

1 point (clarity): The explanation is clearly written

98. Marbles. $\frac{1}{3} > \frac{2}{7}$ can be determined by LCD, where $\frac{7}{21} > \frac{6}{21}$. Or express both fractions as decimals using a calculator and $.\overline{33} >$ 0.2857142.

Rubric: 3 possible points

1 point (content): Realize need to convert to LCD or decimals

1 point (content): Recognize pattern ($\frac{7}{21} > \frac{6}{21}$)

1 point (clarity): Explanation is clearly written

99. 6; 12; 18; 24; 30. The formula is 6 times the neighborhood number or 6N.

Rubric: 4 possible points

1 point (content): Realize that there are 6 nests in neighborhood 1

1 point (content): Realize that as the neighborhood number increases by one from the last neighborhood number, 6 more nests will be added to the total number of nests in the neighborhood.

1 point (content): Each answer is correct

1 point (clarity): The explanation is clearly written

100. 101. The set is made up of number names that begin with a vowel.

101. If player A says 89, Player B cannot win. Player B must add at least 1 and no more than 10, meaning that the sum when Player B finishes is somewhere between 90 and 99 inclusive. No matter what value Player B adds, Player A is now able to add a value that will give the sum of 100. Similarly, if Player A says 78, Player B cannot win because Player B must add at least 1 and no more than 10, meaning that the sum when Player B finishes is somewhere between 79 and 88 inclusive. No matter what value Player B adds, Player A is now able to add a value that will give the sum of 89, which is known to guarantee a win for Player A. The same logic can be used to define a sequence of numbers

that will guarantee a win for Player A (1, 12, 23, 34, 45, 56, 67, 78, 89). Another way to determine the first number that will guarantee a winner is to divide the desired sum (100 in this case) by the sum of the smallest and largest possible addends (1 + 10 in this case).

102. 529; 1000. Since the middle value in an odd-numbered row will be the square of the row number, the middle entry in the 23rd row is $23^2 = 529$.

The sum of all the values in each row is the row number cubed. For example, the values in the second row are 3 and 5. Their sum is 8, which is 2^3, so the sum of the values in the tenth row is $10^3 = 1000$.

Rubric: 3 possible points

1 point (content): Recognize the pattern of cubing a row number to get the sum

1 point (content): Recognize that the middle entry in the odd-numbered rows is the row number squared

1 point (content): Correct arithmetic

1 point (clarity): The explanation is clearly written

103. 8. Since the average age is 11, the total age has to be 33. Take out the 15-year oldest and the 10-year median and you are left with 8.

Rubric: 3 possible points

1 point (content): Proper interpretation of mean and median in the problem

1 point (content): Correct arithmetic

1 point (clarity): The explanation is clearly written

104. 21,000,000

The total number of calls that can be handled in one hour is 700,000 x 25 or 17,500,000. 5% of those are handled incorrectly or, 875,000 calls are handled incorrectly each hour. 875,000 x 24 gives 21,000,000 in one 24-hour period.

Rubric: 3 possible points

1 point (content): Realize the number of incorrect calls per hour is 5% of 700,000 x 25 = 875,000

1 point (content): Realize the need to multiply by 24 hours to get the total number of incorrect calls

1 point (clarity): The explanation is clearly written

105.   1235, 427, 2620

Height is Tower name + 1.

Wing is Tower name.

Total cubes is (3 times the Tower name) + 1.

106.   4N, 2D. First Sunday of each month in 2001

107.   About 44.8 degrees Celsius OR about 80.6 degrees Fahrenheit, depending upon how the conversions are done.

$$F = (\frac{9}{5})C + 32$$

$$= (\frac{9}{5})(-17) + 32$$

$$= -(\frac{153}{5}) + 32$$

$$= -30.6 + 32$$

$$= 1.4 \text{ So, converting } -17 \text{ C to F gives } +1.4 \text{ F.}$$

Subtract to get the difference, 82 – 1.4 = 80.6 F.

$$C = (\frac{5}{9})(F - 32)$$

$$= (\frac{5}{9})(82 - 32)$$

$$= (\frac{5}{9})(50)$$

$$= (\frac{250}{9})$$

$$= 27.77 \text{ or } 27.8 \text{ So, converting } 82° \text{ F to C gives } 27.8° \text{ C.}$$

Subtract to get the difference, 27.8 – (–17) = 44.8 C.

Note: We do not believe in converting between the two temperatures. Give both measurements in Fahrenheit or both measurements in Celsius and be done with it. Most authorities adopt a similar position. The curriculum and tests, however, still ask questions that require students to convert between measurement systems.

Recall the news story in April of 2000 about a Mars orbiter crashing because calculations were done partially in metric and partially in inch, foot, and pound, and no one made the conversions. Based upon that, we thought this might be appropriate.

108.   32%. The first item was purchased for $36 (40% of 60) and the second cost $32 (20% of 40) for a total cost of $68. That means you saved $32 off $100 or 32%.

Rubric: 6 possible points

1 point (content): Realize the need to find 40% of $60

1 point (content): Realize the need to find 20% of $40

1 point (content): Realize the need to add $36 and $32

1 point (content): Realize the need to add $60 and $40

1 point (content): Realize the need to compare $68 to 100

1 point (clarity): The explanation is clearly written

109.   70. The numerals by the points indicate the number of different (and shortest) "legal" routes that could be taken to get to that point.

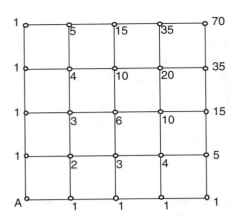

For example, to get to the point named 2 in the smallest square with A, you could go right and up, or you could go up and then right. To get to the point named 6 from A, you could go right, up, right, and up; right, up, up, and right; right, right, up, and up; up, right, up, and right; up, up, right, and right; or up, right, right, and up.

Data could be gathered and analyzed for patterns to arrive at the answer.

110. Each line describes the numeric content of the line above it. There are four ones (4 1), one two (1 2), two threes (2 3), and one four (1 4) in the last line so the next line is

    4 1 1 2 2 3 1 4

The next one after that would be three ones, two twos, one three, and two fours giving

    3 1 2 2 1 3 2 4

Note: This problem can be done other ways. For example, the values can be taken in the order they appear. Doing that, the first four lines would be the same, derived by reading the previous line. However, the fifth line would be different with this new pattern since it would read 132114.

Rubric: 3 possible points

1 point (content): Recognize the pattern

1 point (content): Correct expression of the next line

1 point (clarity): The explanation is clearly written

111. 3780 degrees. Plug and chug

OR

List the values for the angle total in increasing order, recognize the pattern, and apply the pattern until an N-gon with 23 sides is done. For each added side (angle), add 180 degrees.

OR

(N–2)(180) where N is the number of sides in the N-gon.

Note: N-gon is a different way of referring to polygons (closed figure made up of line segments). It replaces a collection of common names that need to be remembered (triangle (3-gon), quadrilateral (4-gon), pentagon (5-gon), hexagon (6-gon), heptagon (7-gon), octagon (8-gon), etc. Use of N-gon certainly simplifies the naming situation. The students should still learn the commonly named figures (triangle, quadrilateral, octagon, hexagon, and octagon) but notice the "gon" part of most of those names.

Concave and convex figures can cause difficulties for some students.

Your students will probably not use the algebraic approach to solve this problem because they do not have those skills. However, the thought process involved is the same, even without the variable. Doing problems like this is a critical first step toward developing those necessary algebra skills.

This is also a good example of a multistep problem that students need to become efficient at solving.

112. $15. $100 – $25 = $75.

    20% of $75 = $15

113. 5, 3, 2. Each number represents the number of letters used to make up the Roman Numerals, beginning with one and counting up one at a time. In other words, I, II, III, IV, V would be represented in the sequence by 1, 2, 3, 2, 1. The 18th Roman Numeral is XVIII, which is made up of 5 letters. The 19th Roman Numeral, XIX has 3 letters and the 20th is XX, which has 2.

114. 28.57142%. You pay $90 for the shoes and $160 for the skates for a total of $250 spent instead of $350. $350 − $250 = $100, the amount of money saved. $\frac{100}{350}$ = 0.2857142 or 28.57142%.

Rubric: 5 possible points

1 point (content): Recognize the need to get each price first

1 point (content): Recognize the need to add purchase prices

1 point (content): Recognize the need to subtract total purchases price from the total asking price

1 point (content): Correct arithmetic

1 point (clarity): The explanation is clearly written

115. 10 ways

1 Red. **1** Blue.

1 with 5 Reds and a Blue. **1** with 5 Blues and a Red.

2 with 4 Reds and 2 Blues (blue adjacent)

2 with 4 Blues and 2 Reds (blue opposite)

2 with 3 Blues and 3 Reds

116. A right ankle

Note: Many students groan at riddles like this, but they do get the point. More significantly, they frequently ask the riddle of others, which can stimulate some positive conversations about the study of mathematics.

117. 6009. The digits 0, 1, 6, and 9 have rotational symmetry.

Rubric: 2 possible points

1 point (content): Realize the next value has to start with a 6

1 point (content): Realize 6009 is the smallest value giving rotational symmetry

118. A rect-bus (wrecked bus) OR, a rectangle that is a rhombus, which can be considered a square.

Note: Many students groan at riddles like this, but they do get the point. More significantly, they frequently ask the riddle of others, which can stimulate some positive conversations about the study of mathematics.

119. Yes. Three small pens are inside a larger pen. The larger pen has 9 ostriches and the 3 smaller pens each contain 3 ostriches.

For example:

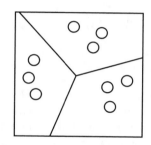

120. J, M, or W.

"O" is 3 letters before "S." Count three letters before "N" and get "J."

OR

Fold the letter S in half horizontally and you get an O.

Fold N in half horizontally and one could argue that the result is M if the fold is toward the top.

OR

Fold N in half horizontally and one could argue that the result is W if the fold is toward the bottom.

Note: It is important that students be given an opportunity to use flexible thinking. The multitude of potential responses to this question can provide additional development for students. If a student gets one answer, encourage her to search for additional ones.

Rubric: 2 possible points

1 point (content): An acceptable pattern is found

1 point (clarity): The explanation is clearly written

121. 10. If there were 2 teams, they would play one game. If there were 3 teams, they would play 3 games (AB, AC, BC). If there were 4 teams, they would play 6 games (AB, AC, AD, BC, BD, CD). If there were 5 teams, they would play 10 games (AB, AC, AD, AE, BC, BD, BE, CD, CE, DE).

Adding a third team adds 2 games. Adding a fourth team adds 3 games for a total of 6. Adding a fifth team adds 4 games for a total of ten. Each additional team will add the next consecutive counting number of games to the total. The formula would be $\dfrac{N(N-1)}{2}$ where N stands for the number of teams in the tournament.

This problem could also be solved using geometry. Use a point to represent an individual and then count the number of segments necessary to join the points in all possible ways.

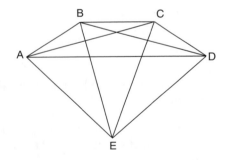

Note: This is like the handshake problem where each individual in a room shakes hands with every other person in the room. Each shake counts as one shake, not a shake for Person A and a shake for Person B.

122. It was beside (an) acute angle!

Note: Many students groan at riddles like this, but they do get the point. More significantly, they frequently ask the riddle of others, which can stimulate some positive conversations about the study of mathematics.

123. X top left corner, O bottom right corner.

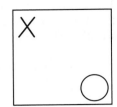

X alternates back and forth between the top left and bottom right corner as you go from left to right.

O goes counterclockwise one corner at a time as the sequence progresses from left to right.

Rubric: 4 possible points

1 point (content): Recognize the pattern for the Xs

1 point (content): Recognize the pattern for the Os

1 point (content): Recognize the blending of the patterns

1 point (clarity): The explanation is clearly written

124. 3456 sq. cm.

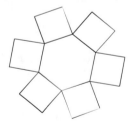

The regular hexagon perimeter of 144 cm. means each side is 24 cm. long ($\dfrac{144}{6}$). That means the area of each square is 576 sq. cm. (24 x 24). But, there are 6 squares so the total area is 6 x (576 sq. cm.) = 3456 sq. cm.

125. Catch planes

Note: Many students groan at riddles like this, but they do get the point. More significantly, they frequently ask the riddle of others, which can stimulate some positive conversations about the study of mathematics.

126. The g-raph

Note: Many students groan at riddles like this, but they do get the point. More significantly, they frequently ask the riddle of others, which can stimulate some positive conversations about the study of mathematics.

127. 25 rectangles. Squares are also rectangles. There are nine 1 by 1 rectangles (squares), ten 1 by 2 rectangles, four 1 by 3 rectangles, and two 2 by 2 rectangles (squares). So, you have 9 + 10 + 4 + 2 = 25.

Rubric: 6 possible points:

1 point (content): Recognize that squares are rectangles

1 point (content): Recognize pattern for 1 by 2 rectangles

1 point (content): Recognize pattern for 1 by 3 rectangles

1 point (content): Recognize pattern for 2 by 2 squares

1 point (content): Recognize all patterns

1 point (clarity): The explanation is clearly written

128. Rectangle. The diameters AC and BD will always bisect each other. That means that you will always have a rectangle for any chord AB that is not a diameter.

Note: Some students might make a square and, therefore, state the answer is a square. While that is true, it is a special case. Since all squares are rectangles, the square response is included in the rectangle response. This would be a great time to discuss the idea that all squares are rectangles, but not all rectangles are squares.

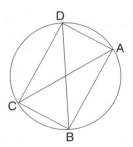

Rubric: 3 possible points:

1 point (content): Diagram is done correctly

1 point (content): Rectangle is given as the answer—not square, quadrilateral, parallelogram, or polygon. (Even though, technically, they are true, rectangle is the most specific.)

1 point (clarity): The explanation is clearly written

129. Answer varies. (I'll tell you tomorrow.) (Delay Thanksgiving Day.)

Note: This is an opportunity for the students to show acceptable creativity and also realize that there is not always one right answer to a problem.

130. 498,000.

131. VIII. Using Roman numerals, thirteen is XIII. If you use a horizontal line segment to divide the top and bottom of XIII you get VIII on top and /\III on the bottom. VIII is 8 in Roman Numerals.

132. 37.5% or 40%. 24 out of the 64 squares have checkers on them to start. This converts to 0.375 or 37.5%

OR

In International Draughts (checkers), 40 pieces sit on a board of 100 squares, which is 40.0 percent coverage.

133. 1. Boys ratio is $\frac{5}{12}$ or 0.416666

2. Girls ratio is $\frac{8}{18}$ or 0.444444

3. Girls because 0.44444 > 0.416666

Also, $\frac{8}{18} > \frac{5}{12}$. If students use fractions, they need to convert $\frac{5}{12}$ and $\frac{8}{18}$ to equivalent fractions that have the same denominator. One way to get the common denominator is to list the multiples of 12 (12, 24, 36, 48, 60…) and 18 (18, 36, 54, 72,…) and then find the smallest common value of 36. Thus, $\frac{5}{12} =$

$\frac{15}{36}$ and $\frac{8}{18} = \frac{16}{36}$. Since the denominators are the same, $\frac{16}{36} > \frac{15}{36}$, and the girls ratio is greater than the boys'.

Rubric: 4 possible points:

1 point (content): Identify the ratio for the boys

1 point (content): Identify the ratio for the girls

1 point (content): Determine that the girls ratio is larger

1 point (clarity): The explanation is clearly written

134. $8\frac{1}{2}$ hours. The tendency is to divide 18 by 2, getting 9. However, the first pill is taken at the beginning of the time period, or at time zero. So the second one is taken at the first half hour, the third at the first hour, etc. There are no pills left to be taken at the 9th hour.

135. 18. $\frac{24}{6} \times 4 - 1 + 3 = 18$

136. 0.5. This could be expressed as $\frac{32}{64}$, $\frac{8}{16}$, $\frac{4}{8}$, $\frac{2}{4}$, or $\frac{1}{2}$.

Rubric: 5 possible points

1 point (content): Recognize that the largest shaded region is $\frac{1}{4}$ of the total

1 point (content): Recognize that the second largest shaded region has two squares, each $\frac{1}{16}$, and combined, $\frac{1}{8}$ of the total (or half of the area of the previous square)

1 point (content): Recognize that the third largest shaded region has 8 squares, each $\frac{1}{64}$, and combined, $\frac{1}{8}$ of the total (or half of the area of the previous square)

1 point (content): The arithmetic is correct

1 point (clarity): The explanation is clearly written

137.

6	52,596,000 blinks	53, nearest million
7	61,362,000	61
8	70,128,000	70
9	78,894,000	79
10	87,660,000	88
11	96,426,000	96
12	105,192,000	105
13	113,958,000	114

Y = year (365.25 days in a year)

Awake = $\frac{2}{3}$ of day

24 = hours in day

60 = minutes in hour

25 = blinks per minute

Total Blinks = $(Y)(365.25)(\frac{2}{3})(24)(60)(25)$

138. Any one is acceptable: 63421, 21210, 42211, 42420, 63212, 63630, 84213, 84422, 84631, 84840, 21001, 42002, 63003, 84004.

A lot of these would be eliminated if digits had to be unique within the answer.

139. $2\frac{1}{2}$ inches. Put the books on a bookshelf in order with volume 1 as the leftmost book and volume three the rightmost. As you look at the books on the shelf, page one of volume one is the rightmost page of volume one and the last page of volume three is the leftmost page of volume three. Therefore, the worm needs to eat through only one cover of volume 1 ($\frac{1}{8}$), 2 covers and the inside of volume 2 ($\frac{1}{8}$ + 2 + $\frac{1}{8}$), and one cover of volume three

$(\frac{1}{8})$ for a total of $\frac{1}{8} + \frac{1}{8} + 2 + \frac{1}{8} + \frac{1}{8} = 2\frac{4}{8}$

$= 2\frac{1}{2}$ inches.

Note: Some children might argue that the books should be arranged differently. Some books are read from right to left and arranged on a shelf with volume 1 on the right as you look at the shelf. In that case, the bookworm would go $6\frac{1}{2}$ inches.

Rubric: 3 possible points

1 point (content): Recognize the correct arrangement of books

1 point (content): Correct arithmetic and answer

1 point (clarity): The explanation is clearly written

140. $\frac{1}{2} + \frac{1}{3} + \frac{1}{6} = 1$. This is the only set of three different unit fractions that will give a sum of one.

A perfect number has the sum of its factors (excluding itself) equaling that number. Six is the first perfect number and the sum of its factors (1, 2, 3, and 6) excluding itself is $1 + 2 + 3 = 6$. This idea of perfect numbers is the clue to the solution. The denominators are the factors of the perfect number other than 1.

The next perfect number is 28, and its factors are 1, 2, 4, 7, 14, and 28 and $\frac{1}{2} + \frac{1}{4} + \frac{1}{7} + \frac{1}{14} + \frac{1}{28} = 1$

The next perfect number is 496. There are fewer than 40 known perfect numbers at the time of this writing. The number of fractions of a perfect number increases with the magnitude of the number, making $\frac{1}{2} + \frac{1}{3} + \frac{1}{6} = 1$ the only possible solution for this question.

141. 2. $\frac{(10 \times 2) + 6 - 2}{12} = 2$

142. 8. $\frac{3 \times 60}{6} - 24 + 2 = 8$

143. $\frac{5}{9}$

$\frac{3}{7}X = \frac{5}{21}$

$X = (\frac{5}{21}) \div (\frac{3}{7})$

$X = (\frac{5}{21})(\frac{7}{3})$

$X = \frac{5}{9}$

Note: Your students will probably not use the algebraic approach to solve this problem because they do not have those skills. However, the thought process involved is the same, even without the variable. Doing problems like this is a critical first step toward developing those necessary algebra skills.

When this problem is done nonalgebraically, the solution is very similar. Interpreting "$\frac{3}{7}$ of what fraction is" gives the idea that some fraction is multiplied by $\frac{3}{7}$, and you are looking for that fraction. You know from the problem that the answer has to be $\frac{5}{21}$ after the multiplication is completed. A similar problem would be 3 times what number is 21, which would be solved by dividing 21 by 3, giving 7 as the missing factor. Using that same approach here, the solution is determined by dividing $\frac{5}{21}$ by $\frac{3}{7}$, giving $(\frac{5}{21})(\frac{7}{3})$ or $\frac{5}{9}$.

144. $160. Excluding the bottom there will be a total of 32 faces (10 on the left face, 10 on the right face, 4 on the back, 4 on the front, and 4 that will be stepped on). 32 x $4.99 = $159.68. Rounded to the nearest dollar, this gives $160.

145. 18.75%. Make the garden a rectangle. Tomatoes take half of that. The broccoli takes a fourth of what is left or $\frac{1}{8}$ of the original plot. That means the remaining area at this point is $\frac{3}{8}$ of the original plot. The lettuce takes half of that remaining $\frac{3}{8}$ or $\frac{3}{16}$. But that leaves $\frac{3}{16}$ for the cauliflower.

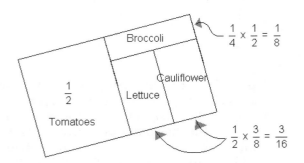

146. 3, 4, and 5. Guess and check. 3 + 4 + 5 = 12 and (3)(4)(5)=60. 12=(0.2)(60)

147. 114.07712 years, 114 to nearest year.

$$1,000,000 \text{ hours } \times \frac{1 \text{ day}}{24 \text{ hours}} \times \frac{1 \text{ year}}{365.25 \text{ days}} = 114.07712 \text{ years}$$

148. 4 are listed below. There may be others.

$$\frac{3 + 4 - 7 + 6}{\frac{10}{5}} = 3$$

$$10\left(\frac{3}{5}\right)\left(\frac{7}{6}\right) - 4 = 3$$

$$\frac{3(10) + 4 + 5}{7 + 6} = 3$$

$$\frac{3(4) + 5 + 6 + 7}{10} = 3$$

Rubric: 3 possible points

1 point (content): Correct placement of all values.

1 point (content): Use of all values given

1 point (clarity): The explanation is clearly written.

149. 0.48958333

square + rectangle + triangle + 3 little squares

$$= \frac{1}{4} + \left(\frac{1}{2}\right)\left(\frac{1}{4}\right) + \left(\frac{1}{8}\right)\left(\frac{1}{4}\right) + \left(\frac{3}{9}\right)\left(\frac{1}{4}\right)$$

$$= \frac{1}{4} + \frac{1}{8} + \frac{1}{32} + \frac{3}{36}$$

$$= \frac{141}{288}$$

$$= \frac{47}{96}$$

$$= 0.48958333$$

150. 4. $1\frac{1}{3} = \frac{4}{3}$ (this makes the solution easier to see)

$$\frac{4}{3} + X = \left(\frac{4}{3}\right)X$$

but $\left(\frac{4}{3}\right)X = \frac{4X}{3}$, so

$$\frac{4}{3} + X - X = \left(\frac{4}{3}\right)X - X$$

$$\frac{4}{3} = \frac{4X}{3} - X$$

$$\frac{4}{3} = \frac{4X}{3} - \frac{3X}{3}$$

$$\frac{4}{3} = \frac{X}{3}$$

151. $\frac{17}{18}$ or $\frac{34}{36}$ or 0.944. Three comes up two ways out of 36 possible results: You roll a (1, 2) or (2, 1). So, not rolling these two would be $\frac{34}{36}$.

Rubric: 3 possible points

1 point (content): Recognize the answer is not

$$\frac{2}{36}$$

1 point (content): Recognize there are only 2 ways out of 36 to get 3

1 point (clarity): The explanation is clearly written

152. $\frac{189}{1 + 8 + 9}$ = 10.5. Since A cannot be zero, it must be 1 because the larger A is, the greater the numerator and greater the value of the fraction. By using 8 and 9, you can maximize the value of the denominator and

$$\frac{189}{1 + 8 + 9} < \frac{198}{1 + 9 + 8} .$$

Rubric: 4 possible points

1 point (content): Realize A = 1 to make numerator as small as possible

1 point (content): Realize that B = 8 or 9 and C = 9 or 8 to make denominator as large as possible

1 point (content): Realize

$$\frac{189}{1 + 8 + 9} < \frac{198}{1 + 9 + 8}$$

1 point (clarity): The explanation is clearly written

153. $\frac{1}{4} = \frac{4392}{17568} = \frac{5796}{23184} = \frac{7956}{31824}$. This is done mostly with guess and check, but there are some things the students should notice. For example, the ones digit in the denominator of $\frac{4392}{17568}$ is 4 times the ones digit in the numerator of that fraction. In the other two examples, students who remember that 6 x 4 = 24 will have a similar clue. In all three examples, the student should notice that the relation between the thousands digit in the numerator and the ten-thousands and thousands digits in the respective denominators should be in a ratio of about 1 to 4.

154. Tuesday at 48 seconds after 40 minutes after 4 A.M.

$$\frac{1,000,000}{60 \text{ minutes x } 60 \text{ seconds x } 24 \text{ hours}} = 11.57 \text{ days}$$

11.57 days

0.57 days = 13.68 hours which switches from P.M. to A.M. of the next day

0.68 hours = 40.8 minutes

0.8 minutes = 48 seconds

155. Write "*A Bigger One*" on the chalkboard or overhead projector.

Note: Many students groan at questions like this, but they do get the point. More significantly, they frequently ask the question of others, which can stimulate some positive conversations about the study of mathematics.

156. Varies. The key to understanding the problem is focusing on the right information. If we assume it is critical to keep track of the number of people getting on and off the bus, we focus on information that turns out to be unessential. It distracts us from the important information. The answer to the problem is found in the first sentence. You are driving the bus so the color is the color of your eyes.

Note: If you didn't get it right, don't worry. The majority of people don't answer correctly. Students who get this correct have the potential to be good problem solvers.

Rubric: 2 possible points

1 point (content): Recognize irrelevant facts

1 point (clarity): The explanation is clearly written

157. Varies (a sawhorse, rocking horse)

158. I've got problems!

Note: Many students groan at riddles like this, but they do get the point. More significantly, they frequently ask the riddle of others, which can stimulate some positive conversations about the study of mathematics.

159.   6. Draw a picture. The farmer has 5 daughters and one son. The son is a brother to each of the 5 daughters.

160.   E, N, T. The letters stand for the first letters of the words eighth, ninth, tenth

Rubric: 2 possible points

1 point (content): Recognition of the pattern

1 point (clarity): The explanation is clearly written

Note: Many students groan at questions like this, but they do get the point. More significantly, they frequently ask the question of others, which can stimulate some positive conversations about the study of mathematics.

161.   E, N, T. one, two, three, four, five, six, seven, <u>eight</u>, <u>nine</u>, <u>ten</u>. The letters stand for the first letters of the counting numbers from one to ten.

Rubric: 2 possible points

1 point (content): Recognize the pattern

1 point (clarity): The explanation is clearly written

Note: Many students groan at questions like this, but they do get the point. More significantly, they frequently ask the question of others, which can stimulate some positive conversations about the study of mathematics.

162.   25. The trees on the right side when going to town are the same trees that are appearing on the left side when returning.

Note: a good way to model this problem is to have some students line up as trees along a "street" while others "go" to town and back along that street.

163.   Math-a-chusetts

Note: Many students groan at riddles like this, but they do get the point. More significantly, they frequently ask the riddle of others, which can stimulate some positive

conversations about the study of mathematics.

164.   Tricky problems

Note: Many students groan at riddles like this, but they do get the point. More significantly, they frequently ask the riddle of others, which can stimulate some positive conversations about the study of mathematics.

165.   They are arranged alphabetically by their number words.

Rubric: 2 possible points

1 point (content): Recognize the pattern

1 point (clarity): The explanation is clearly written

Note: Many students groan at questions like this, but they do get the point. More significantly, they frequently ask the question of others, which can stimulate some positive conversations about the study of mathematics.

166.   BANANA. Take out S, I, X, L, E, T, T, E, R, S.

Rubric: 2 possible points

1 point (content): Recognize the pattern

1 point (clarity): The explanation is clearly written

Note: It is important to give students problems like this in order to encourage them to think about unusual directions or patterns.

167.   No. If he is living, he won't be buried!

Note: Many students groan at questions like this, but they do get the point. More significantly, they frequently ask the question of others, which can stimulate some positive conversations about the study of mathematics.

168.   Varies. The wizard must keep track of the NUMBER OF TIMES the teacher points to numbers on the board.

169.   Because seven eight (ate) nine

Note: Many students groan at riddles like this, but they do get the point. More significantly, they frequently ask the riddle of others, which can stimulate some positive conversations about the study of mathematics.

170. With three strikes of the bat—he is out! Students may argue that it could be a live bat. Then they may brainstorm for other solutions.

Note: Many students groan at questions like this, but they do get the point. More significantly, they frequently ask the question of others, which can stimulate some positive conversations about the study of mathematics.

171. Your age

Note: Many students groan at riddles like this, but they do get the point. More significantly, they frequently ask the riddle of others, which can stimulate some positive conversations about the study of mathematics.

172. JUST ONE WORD

173. The match

Note: Many students groan at questions like this, but they do get the point. More significantly, they frequently ask the question of others, which can stimulate some positive conversations about the study of mathematics.

174. t e n h o r s e s. *tenhorses* has 9 letters in it. Spell the words, using one letter per stall. This trick question has generated a lot of discussion and stimulates divergent thinking. The objective of this problem is more than just finding the answer.

175. The rat took its own 2 ears and 1 ear of corn each time it left the barn. If the rat carried only 1 ear of corn per day, it would take the rat 9 days to remove the 9 ears of corn from the barn.

Note: Many students groan at questions like this, but they do get the point. More significantly, they frequently ask the question of others, which can stimulate some positive conversations about the study of mathematics.

176. 11. You would count the fingers and thumb on one hand 10, 9, 8, 7, 6. When you finish that, you are at 6. Now add 5 for the other hand and $6 + 5 = 11$. This happens because when you count from 10 down on the first hand you essentially name the digits as 10, 9, 8, 7, and 6. There are still only 5 digits on that hand. However, by ending with the name 6 and then adding 5 for the digits on the other hand, you appear to end up with 11 fingers. The counting is a naming process only. The names have no impact on the total number of fingers.

177. 0. Pine trees do not have acorns.

Note: Many students groan at questions like this, but they do get the point. More significantly, they frequently ask the question of others, which can stimulate some positive conversations about the study of mathematics.

178. Four and nine. Cross out the letters that form "S E V E N L E T T E R S" and you will leave F, O, U, R, N, I, N, and E.

Note: Many students will groan when they see this solution and yet they will be very quick to show the problem to someone else. They also learn to be a little more flexible in their approach to problems.

179. 55. 2 people have 1 shake; 3 people (named A, B, and C) have 3 shakes (AB (A and B shake), AC, BC); 4 people (named A, B, C, and D) have 6 shakes (AB, AC, AD, BC, BD, CD); 5 have 10; 6 have 15; 7 have 21; 8 have 28; 9 have 36; 10 have 45; 11 have 55.

OR

if N = the number of people shaking hands, the formula $\dfrac{N(N-1)}{2}$ gives the total—in this example

$$\frac{11(11-1)}{2} = \frac{11(10)}{2}$$
$$= 55$$

The numbers for each group of people could be listed and analyzed for patterns. Some students should recognize the pattern of adding consecutive counting numbers to the sums.

People	Shakes	Number added
2	1	
3	3	2
4	6	3
5	10	4

etc.

Geometrically, each vertex represents a person. Join the vertices with all possible straight segments.

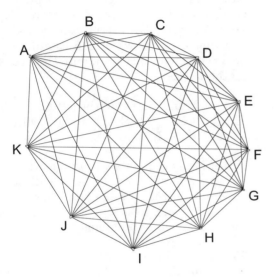

180. T E N. Add one horizontal segment centered above the first vertical segment to make a T, add three horizontal segments to the right of the second vertical segment to make an E, and add a diagonal segment going from top left to lower right between the last two vertical segments to make an N.